The Story of the U.S. Air Force is an exciting story, filled with important achievements and peopled by men of vision and courage.

Here are stirring accounts of the Wright brothers' first powered flight in 1903; of the role aviation played in World War I; and of "the golden age of aviation" when American pilots made daring flights and set record after record. Here too are the thrilling air battles and bombing missions of World War II; the Berlin airlift; today's minute men of the air; and the new Air Force Academy.

In addition, the reader will meet the reckless, daring, skillful men who made history in the sky—Eddie Rickenbacker, Billy Mitchell, Jimmy Doolittle, Curtis LeMay, to name only a few—as well as such famous planes as the P-38 Lightning, P-47 Thunderbolt, B-17 Flying Fortress and F-86 Sabrejet.

The Story of the

U.S. AIR FORCE

The Story of the
U.S.
AIR
FORCE

BY ROBERT D. LOOMIS

Illustrated with photographs

RANDOM HOUSE · NEW YORK

The pictures included in this book are official U.S. Air Force photographs, with the following exceptions: Boeing Airplane Company (from the collection of Martin Caidin), page 2; Martin Caidin, 167 bottom; United Press International, endpapers, ii-iii, 88, 131; U.S. Navy, 81; Wide World Photos, 122 top, 140 bottom.

All rights reserved under International and Pan-American Copyright Conventions. Published in New York by Random House, Inc., and simultaneously in Toronto, Canada, by Random House of Canada, Limited. Library of Congress Catalog Card Number: 59–8476
Manufactured in the United States of America

For my mother and father

CONTENTS

The United States Air Force is the youngest of our nation's armed services. A little more than fifty years ago it was only a small, unimportant part of the Army Signal Corps. Today it plays a predominant role in the defense of our country and shares equal stature with its older companion services, the Army and the Navy.

From the beginning, the unique strength of the Air Force has come from the courage, vision and actions of its individual members. In The Story of the Air Force *Robert D. Loomis has rightly chosen to tell this dramatic narrative in terms of the airmen who lived it. Their feats demonstrate the indomitable spirit that has made the United States Air Force so important in the world today. They make inspiring reading for young airmen and spacemen of the future.*

Curtis E. LeMay

GENERAL, U.S. AIR FORCE

VICE CHIEF OF STAFF

The Story of the

U.S. AIR FORCE

1957

B-52s
Around
the World

More than four hundred years ago the earth was circled for the first time. It took the small 60-foot *Vittoria* almost three years to complete the dangerous journey. Most of the members of the expedition, including its daring leader, Ferdinand Magellan, did not return at all.

The earth has been circumnavigated many times since Magellan's historic voyage, but perhaps no later attempt has rivaled the Great Navigator's in importance until the one which began on January 16, 1957.

It was just after noon. Five huge ships—ships of the sky this time—rolled slowly down the runway at Castle Air Force Base in California. They were B-52 "Stratofortresses," the giant jet-bombers of the United States Air Force Strategic Air Command. Magellan could not have imagined them in his wildest dreams. Their sloping, swept-back wings, which were highly flexible, measured 185 feet tip to tip—more than three times the length of the stubby *Vittoria.* Each B-52 carried eight shrieking jet pods slung beneath its wings, giving it the power of fifty-six Diesel railroad engines. With this tremendous thrust the mammoth 200-ton bomber could reach a speed of 650 miles per hour, and it carried fuel enough to fly more than 6,000 miles.

The forty-five men inside the B-52s, under the command of Major General Archie Old, Jr., had been told where they were going only hours before.

That is the way the Strategic Air Command does things: its planes and men must be ready to fly anywhere and everywhere at a moment's notice. Still, what these fliers had been told they were going to do today was a challenge to excite even the most hardened veteran.

The men had been called to the briefing room as usual. There was a guard at the door; the preparation for this mission called for top security. As soon as they were all seated the lights were turned out. In front of them was a gigantic illuminated map of the whole world. Across the map were lines drawn with tape and luminescent paint. The men had seen a map like this many times before, but never when the lines connected all the way across it so that really they formed a continuous unbroken band. They understood immediately what it meant. They were going to do something never done before. They were going to fly completely around the world nonstop in their jet-bombers.

Of course men had flown around the world before. In 1924 two U. S. Army Air Service biplanes had done it in 175 days, and there had been many flights since. As a matter of fact, in 1949 the commander of today's lead B-52, Lieutenant Colonel James Morris, had flown in the first plane to make the journey nonstop, the propeller-driven B-50, *Lucky Lady II.* She took almost four days.

But this was different. SAC had said it could strike anywhere in the world at any time to defend America. And what better way was there to demonstrate this to everyone—and particularly those who might think of attacking us—than to send our standard operational SAC bombers on a routine mission non-stop around the world? And they must not fail.

Lieutenant Colonel Morris lifted his B-52 off the runway at 1:00 P.M. The others followed, stringing out in loose formation behind the leader.

High over America their white contrails marked a dramatic eastward course—over the Midwest, the Great Lakes, Canada . . .

Over Labrador the first mishap occurred. One of the bombers developed mechanical trouble and had to drop out. Actually such an eventuality had been foreseen and prepared for. As a matter of fact one of the four remaining aircraft was still considered a "spare" and when the flight reached Africa it was ordered north to land in England.

So far the men had not seen another plane of any kind, nor would they during the entire trip so long as they remained at their cruise level of 35- to 50,000 feet. But when the B-52s began to nose down to more normal altitudes all eyes strained ahead for the first rendezvous. Suddenly, in the sky below, Colonel Morris sighted the speck he had been looking for. As he closed in on the new plane it gradually took on the shape of SAC's special "stratotanker," the KC-97.

Like all SAC pilots, Colonel Morris had refueled in mid air countless times, but no good pilot ever relaxes while such a complex operation is going on. It takes all his skill. The prop-driven KC-97 tanker is a fast plane, but nowhere nearly as fast as the B-52. (The day would come when the Air Force would have jet tankers.) The big bomber must slow down as much as possible and carefully swing up under the rear of the tanker. From the tail of the KC-97 projects a long boom. Colonel Morris, following precise instructions from the tanker, flew his

200 tons of airplane closer and closer until the boom fitted into his bomber's tanks. Then, locked together thousands of feet in the air, the two planes began the transfer of the vital fuel. Through the boom, the tanker pumped a mixture of kerosene and gasoline into the bomber at the rate of 600 gallons a minute. All the while Colonel Morris followed the progress of the complicated operation by interpreting an intricate system of signal lights on the belly of the KC-97.

Suddenly he saw the sign that the refueling was over; on signal the planes pulled apart, the B-52 heading for the heavens again, the KC-97 for the ground, more fuel—and another rendezvous.

The meeting was repeated several times during the flight, just how many times, or where, SAC won't say. In any case, refueling is a welcome break in the monotony of flying 50,000 feet above the earth. Looking out of the windows the men usually can see nothing but clouds—often only far below them —and the limitless expanse of space. Some of the crew brought along magazines and books to read.

The tail gunner of Colonel Morris' plane read four novels during the trip.

The formation headed across North Africa, Saudi Arabia, the Indian Ocean. . . . On and on they flew, turning a "routine" training mission into a modern miracle.

But no SAC mission is ever complete without its simulated bombing run. This time the target selected was over Malaya, more than halfway around the globe from California. As the big bombers began their runs the bombardiers took over control of the plane. Electronically the air speed, wind drift, height —all the factors which must be considered for accurate high-level bombing—were computed. And then "Bombs away!" Target theoretically destroyed.

And now they were on the last leg of their journey. Heading out across the vast Pacific Ocean, they roared over Guam. The crews were dead tired as the B-52s sped toward home.

Up ahead, the third dawn they had seen on the trip slowly appeared out of the east. Some of the men were puzzled. Their watches told them they had been away from base only about two days. How could they have flown through three nights? Then they figured it out. They had been flying east at a tremendous rate of speed, and since time is told by the passage of the sun, they had lived through three shortened nights, while everyone else on earth had gone through only two.

Suddenly someone called out, "Land, ho!" Up ahead in the morning sunlight was the California coast. The men smiled and congratulated one another. They had made it.

At 10:13 A.M. the formation swept over the field where a crowd had collected. Then the giant B-52s landed exactly one minute apart, a parachute blossoming from the tail of each to slow it down on the runway. They had circled the earth in the record time of only forty-five hours and nineteen minutes.

As they stepped from their aircraft the twenty-six crew members had an unexpected honor waiting for them. At the head of a welcoming committee was none other than General Curtis LeMay, then Commander in Chief of the Strategic Air Command. And as a thirty-piece band joined in the welcome,

General LeMay came forward, shook the hand of each crew member and pinned a medal on him. The men looked down in surprise. The General was presenting each of them with the Distinguished Flying Cross, the highest decoration given by this country for flying.

But each of them knew they had done more than win those coveted medals. They had dramatized to the whole world the fact that SAC and the United States Air Force were the most potent weapons for peace in the world.

It was an impressive achievement from any point of view, but perhaps no more impressive than the tremendous strides aviation had made in the short span of only fifty years. Incredible as it might seem, there were men in that crowd gathered around the B-52 fliers who could remember when the United States had only one airplane; indeed, many could remember a time when man could not fly at all.

1903-1910

The
First
Fliers

In the years just before and after the beginning of the twentieth century, the wizards, tinkerers and inspired dreamers of America—in short, that peculiar individual called the inventor—presented to the world a dazzling procession of amazing devices.

Suddenly man could send his voice for miles

through a tiny wire; he could also "record" it permanently on a small wax cylinder. When they first appeared, some of the inventions that were to change our lives—such as the electric light, motion pictures and the automobile—were so startling (or odd) that neither their inventors nor the public fully understood just how valuable they were. Certainly it is difficult to think of an event more exciting than the invention of a machine that would enable man to fly through the air. Yet when the Wright brothers made their first powered flight at Kitty Hawk in 1903 scarcely anybody noticed it; and most of those who heard about it didn't believe it anyway.

A new era had begun. For the first time in history a heavier-than-air machine with a man in it had lifted itself and its passenger off. the ground and landed safely at a place no lower than its take-off point.

The news was sent out, but the next morning only three newspapers in the whole United States carried the story.

It wasn't that the papers weren't interested in such a story; it was simply that they didn't believe it. Our government didn't believe it either. Wilbur and Orville could not, of course, foresee all the uses to which the airplane would be put in only a few years, but they did think that sports fliers would like it; and certainly the Army could use it for scouting purposes. But when the brothers offered to demonstrate their plane, the Army answered only with a form letter which stated they were not interested. (Actually the Army thought the Wrights were simply another pair of cranks; the government had already invested in one inventor's "flying machine" and the thing had crashed twice. Army officers were not anxious to be held up to ridicule again.)

Europe took the claims of the Wright brothers with a great deal more faith. In fact, several European countries became so enthusiastic that they sent representatives to America to purchase the plane. Luckily this foreign enthusiasm came to the attention of President Theodore Roosevelt and he ordered the matter investigated.

Thus it was that late in 1907 the Army Signal Corps sent out a directive for bids on an air machine which could carry a crew of two, fly faster than forty miles an hour and, of all things, be carried in a four-wheel, mule-driven wagon.

Forty-one bids were received, but out of all of them, of course, only Wilbur and Orville had a plane that could fly.

The tests began at Fort Myer, Virginia, the following year. When Orville took off the crowd gasped. They couldn't believe it. He circled the field, and landed. Reporters who rushed up to him after the flight actually had tears in their eyes. The trials were cut short two weeks later, however, when tragedy struck. Orville was flying with a passenger, Lieutenant Thomas E. Selfridge, when suddenly a propeller cracked and chopped through a vital wire leading to the tail. The plane dived for the ground and crashed. Orville was thrown clear, suffering broken ribs and a fractured hip. Thomas Selfridge was mortally injured and died a few hours later.

He was the first person to be killed in this new Age of Flight.

The following year the Wrights returned to Fort Myer with an improved plane and after several weeks of tests the official military trials began. The smart

Aviation's first fatality: Lieutenant Thomas E. Selfridge dies in the crash of a Wright plane.

little biplane passed each requirement with ease. On the last day a cheering crowd of seven thousand watched Orville and his passenger, Lieutenant Ben Foulois, wing over a ten-mile course at the breathtaking speed of 42.5 miles an hour. The Wright brothers had shown they could deliver exactly what they had promised.

And for $30,000 the Army bought its first flying machine.

The Wrights had also agreed to teach two officers to fly the new contraption, and this they did: after a little more than three hours of instruction apiece, Lieutenants Frank Lahm and Fred Humphreys soloed. Unfortunately only a few days after this triumph these two officers smashed up the plane, though not beyond repair. And on top of this mishap the Army suddenly—and routinely—transferred Lahm and Humphreys back to their original units in the Cavalry and the Engineers.

This left our fledgling air arm with one damaged airplane and no pilots. While the Wright plane was being repaired, the Army decided to shift its flying operations south to the warmer climate of the Texas border. Ben Foulois, whose brief training had taught him how to take off but not how to land, was now the only "flying" officer on duty. He set out to teach himself. Time after time he took off for a short hop, always returning miraculously unharmed— though not as much could be said for the Army's "aerial fleet" with its one plane.

After each disastrous landing, Foulois would write Wilbur and Orville what had happened, and they would reply telling him what he had done wrong. Thus he became the first correspondence-school pilot in history. More than that, Foulois had to pay some of his expenses out of his own pocket. The Army had allotted only $150 for repairs and gasoline for the whole year!

With his sixty-one flights, Ben Foulois kept the Aeronautical Division of the Army Signal Corps in business; for as late as 1911 the United States military forces had only one airplane and one pilot.

1911-1917

Early Days
in the
Bird Cage

On an April night in 1911, a handsome young man
sat up wide awake as the train he was riding on
sped through the darkness toward Dayton, Ohio. He
did not know it then, of course, but thirty years later
he would be a full general in command of the largest
air force ever created in history. Right now he was

only a lieutenant and he was worried whether he would be able to learn to fly at all. His name was Henry H. Arnold (his friends called him "Hap") and he was on his way to begin training as a pilot with the Wright brothers.

When he arrived in Dayton, Hap Arnold went straight to the Wright factory where he met Wilbur and Orville as well as their assistants. Lieutenant Tom Milling from the 15th Cavalry was to be Arnold's companion student, but there were others training alongside these Army men, including a Navy officer and even a few civilians.

Arnold and Milling began their instruction in the back room of the factory where an old plane was set up on two sawhorses as if in flight. When Hap Arnold saw this complicated structure of wire and struts he understood immediately why some of the early planes were called "bird cages." Someone had once remarked that the easiest way to discover if a wire was broken was to let a bird loose in the plane; if it got out something was wrong. In this battered "crate" this future general of the Air Force learned how the Wrights' plane was controlled (which was, by the way, completely different and more difficult than several other airplanes being manufactured by that time). "A right turn, for instance," Arnold wrote later, "was achieved by pulling a lever back to lift the left wing and simultaneously rotating the hand grip an appropriate number of degrees to the right for right rudder."

These movements did not come naturally while one was sitting in a strange machine which was teetering on two sawhorses, but Arnold mastered them. This was called primary training, and after it came actual flying instruction. By now he was getting the feel of the Wright plane. His log book records that after less than four hours in the air he landed three times "without assistance." Then he soloed. Hap Arnold was a flier.

But in those days a flier still had a great deal to learn. There were many crashes, but no one could figure out why. Once a young naval officer was thrown out of his seat into the air but luckily managed to grasp a wing wire and hang on. After that

21

the fliers strapped themselves in with belts, as all pilots do today. Another time a bug hit Arnold in the eye and he almost crashed. It had never occurred to anyone before that such a thing might happen. From then on all fliers wore goggles.

These fledgling fliers also learned a lot from the experienced Wright brothers. Every Sunday the Wrights invited Lieutenants Arnold and Milling to their home. The two young men never tired of listening to the two former bicycle makers as they told of the exciting years which had brought the miracle of flight to the world.

Then it was time to leave Dayton. Hap Arnold and Tom Milling knew they had a big job ahead of them. Not only were they now the only qualified pilots in the Army (the others had either been transferred or killed), they had to return to College Park Field and teach their own commanding officers how to fly. Luckily the Wright plane had two seats so that in-flight training was not too difficult. Learning to fly in the single-seat plane Glenn Curtiss manufactured in San Diego was a different matter, however. The instructor had to run alongside the plane

22

Lieutenants Henry H. Arnold and Thomas Milling in 1912, just after training at the Wright brothers' school.

yelling advice. Necessarily the first flight the inexperienced pilot made was solo.

During these early years the air arm of the Signal Corps was trying to find its place against heavy opposition. Little money was given to it for operational expenses and there was violent disagreement as to its function. The pilots themselves were trying everything. Hap Arnold set an altitude record—

4,674 feet; a machine gun was fired from a plane piloted by Tom Milling; artillery fire was directed from the air; landings were made at night by the light of burning gasoline drums; Lieutenant B. Q. Jones became the first Army officer to loop a plane; and as early as 1910 small two-pound sandbags, simulating bombs, were dropped on a target.

But all of this was experimental and, for the moment, of no practical value. Moreover it was dangerous. Twelve of the first forty-eight flying officers had been killed. And when the airplane was put to some practical military use, it usually failed. In 1912 two airplanes were sent to Connecticut for maneuvers with ground troops. The most exciting thing that happened was the capture of Ben Foulois by "enemy" troops when he landed in a field to send a telegram telling of the enemy's position.

A more important, but equally unsuccessful, test came in 1916. In March of that year the famous Mexican bandit Pancho Villa raided a small town in New Mexico, killing seventeen Americans. Enraged, our government ordered General John J. Pershing into Mexico to track down Villa and bring him back, dead or alive. With Pershing's force of 15,000 troops went the 1st Aero Squadron, commanded by Ben Foulois, with its eight planes. Its first mission was simply to fly to its advance base at Casa Grandes, Mexico. But the underpowered "Jenny" training planes were not up to it. One crashed, one had to turn back, and the remaining six had to make forced landings in the darkness.

For several weeks the determined pilots tried to carry out the duties assigned to them—carrying mail, delivering messages, and scouting—but it was impossible. The trainers were so underpowered they could not fly over the surrounding mountains. Once Foulois was caught in a rain storm and had to try to fly with his feet completely under water in his cockpit before his motor quit. A little later his plane was almost destroyed by a crowd when he landed to deliver a message to the American consul in Chihuahua City.

In the end only two planes were still operational

and these were in such bad shape that they were ordered condemned.

Admittedly aviation was a new business. There was a lot to be done, and much to learn by trial and error. Nevertheless America, which had given flight to the world, was falling far behind. In Europe World War I was in progress. It had been going on for more than two years and aviation was playing a part of growing importance. The best planes we had were inadequate trainers. They weren't even armed. Several European countries now had thousands of fighter planes which were not only fast and highly maneuverable but also were fitted with machine guns. They even had bombers.

Strangely enough, many Americans, including the military, were not aware of this. Even if they had been, Congress had not given the armed forces enough money to do anything about it. A few American boys, however, were anxious to join the fight—particularly the new war in the air. By special arrangement, so that they wouldn't have to give up their citizenship, they were allowed to join the French Flying Corps.

Their unit soon became famous under the name of the Lafayette Escadrille. Flying French airplanes, but with a skill and bravery all their own, they showed the world that although America might be temporarily behind in the production of aircraft, her fliers were equal to the best of any country.

At the time of the 1st Aero Squadron's fiasco in Mexico, Americans like Kiffin Yates Rockwell, Norman Prince, Victor Chapman, William Thaw, Bert Hall, Raoul Lufbery and scores of others were meeting the best pilots Germany had to offer in deadly dogfights in the skies over Europe. Fifty-one were killed but the Lafayette Escadrille officially destroyed 199 German aircraft. Perhaps more important, the ideals they fought for were the same ones millions of Americans were willing to fight for, and would fight for. On April 6, 1917, Congress declared war on Germany. Now the Lafayette Escadrille would no longer fight alone. Now the deaths of boys like Kiffin Rockwell, Victor Chapman and Norman Prince would not be in vain.

1918

Our
First War
in the Air

The pilots of the 94th "Hat-in-the-Ring" Pursuit Squadron stationed near Toul, France, were excited. For the past few weeks their new commander, Captain Raoul Lufbery of the Lafayette Escadrille, had been teaching them everything he had learned while scoring his seventeen victories. At last he had posted orders for a combat patrol. Tomorrow, April 14, 1918, they were going to fight! The orders said that Captain Peterson, along with Lieutenants Reed Chambers and Edward Rickenbacker, were to take off at dawn and patrol to Saint Mihiel at 16,000 feet; Lieutenants Alan Winslow and Douglas Campbell were to stand by.

As their envious companions watched Chambers and Rickenbacker take off with Captain Peterson in the first all-American patrol of the war, a fog bank slowly closed in on the area. The three fliers did the best they could in the fog, but Chambers became temporarily lost and the others returned to the field low on fuel. Then the sound of two enemy planes was heard overhead. Winslow and Campbell, who were on stand-by, took off immediately.

The whole population of Toul stared upward into the impenetrable haze as the sound of machine-gun fire barked from the sky. Suddenly a German plane plummeted from the fog, out of control. Then another fell near the airfield. Winslow and Campbell had scored the first air victories for an American squadron.

The people of Toul went wild. The Americans were everything it was said they were and more! The wreckage of the two German planes was carted to the town square and a great outdoor party began with the fliers of the 94th as guests of honor.

For Colonel William Mitchell the two victories were the beginning of a dream come true. More than any other man in America in recent years, he had tried to make the Air Service more than just an offshoot of the Signal Corps. "Billy" Mitchell had a vision. He foresaw the day when airpower might be the deciding factor in a war.

He had not always been interested in airplanes; in fact, he planned to make the Army his career. When he was only thirty-two he was appointed to the General Staff. Then World War I broke out. Almost immediately he saw the potential of the airplane, and in 1916 he began to take flying lessons. In March, 1917, he went to the Continent to see this new air war for himself.

It was a different war than almost anyone could have imagined even a few years before. Gone were the "bird cages" and the makeshift efforts at armament. In 1915 the Dutch designing genius Anthony Fokker had worked out a device which could synchronize the rate of fire of a machine gun with the whirling blades of a propeller; soon the German fliers were ruling the skies over No Man's Land. But soon, too, one of Fokker's little monoplanes was shot down by the Allies and the secret was out. Now a new battle began, a battle between the aircraft designers of both sides. They knew that the side that could put up the fastest, most maneuverable planes armed with synchronized machine guns might win the war.

But there was more to it than machines, as Billy Mitchell found out. A new breed of men flew those machines. They were reckless, they were daring, and they were incredibly skillful. They fought to kill but they respected one another. When an honored enemy was downed, it was not unusual for the victor to fly over the lines and drop a wreath at his funeral.

From France came the outstanding Rene Fonck (75 victories) and the romantic Georges Guynemer (53 victories) who had been refused by the army because of poor health but who fought with the fury of ten men. From England there was James Mc-Cudden (58 victories) who was a quiet boy but a superb flier; the great leader "Mick" Mannock (73 victories); and nineteen-year-old Albert Ball (43 victories). From Canada there was Billy Bishop (72 victories) who once shot down twenty-five German planes in twelve days. And from Germany there were men like Oswald Boelcke and Ernst Udet. But above all there was the all-time ace-of-aces, Manfred von Richthofen, who flew an all-red plane and destroyed eighty Allied aircraft before he was killed. These men and scores like them wrote a new chapter in the history of warfare.

All this Billy Mitchell saw. It made him realize how far his country had fallen behind in the air. When the United States entered the war only a month after he had arrived in Europe we had only 200 serviceable planes and not one of these was fit for combat. Our pilots, then, would have to fly foreign ships. Mitchell insisted on testing every type of airplane the French and English wanted our fliers to use. He turned down the early version of the British Sopwith Camel fighter because it had a vicious tendency to spin, and finally settled on the French Nieuport. Later he was able to outfit many of our squadrons with the new French Spad. But Mitchell saw beyond the small single-seat "scouting" planes. Dogfights were dramatic and glamorous, but they alone could not win a war.

Still there was no one who showed more pride in the new American aces than Billy Mitchell himself. There were more and more of them every day, but there were some who stood head and shoulders above the rest.

One who particularly came to his attention was a cowboy from Arizona named Frank Luke. This young flier was doing the seemingly impossible: one after another he was shooting down the Kaiser's valuable observation balloons. "Balloon busting," as it was called, was a dangerous sport. A balloon was easy enough to hit—if you could get close to it. The trouble was that it was protected from below by anti-aircraft and machine guns, and overhead swift German fighter planes circled to pounce on any enemy plane which ventured too near. And yet time after

Lieutenant Frank Luke, the cowboy from Arizona, beside his Spad.

time Frank Luke flew into this death trap.

When Luke first arrived in France he was not very well liked by his fellow pilots. He bragged and he strutted. Things got so bad that when he returned from a patrol claiming he'd shot down a German plane they wouldn't believe him. They nicknamed him "The Arizona Boaster."

But Luke found one friend, a quiet easygoing boy from Massachusetts named Joseph Wehner. With Wehner's help Luke decided he'd go after some observation balloons. *Nobody* could fail to see those giants going down in flames.

Their first day out, Frank Luke got two balloons while his friend protected him from above. Billy Mitchell personally saw this attack; later he counted over fifty bullet holes in each ship. Within a week the new team had blown up nine more balloons and shot down four German airplanes.

The fliers of the 27th Squadron began to look a bit differently at the Arizona Boaster—and they didn't call him that any more.

September 17, 1918, was a red-letter day for Frank Luke, but it cost him dearly. With Wehner covering him he attacked three balloons which had been spying on American lines. Diving through dangerously thick anti-aircraft flak Luke got the first balloon. And then the second. But Joe Wehner was unable to fight off the swarm of German fighters trying to get through to his partner. Luke, seeing that Wehner was in trouble, came to his aid. But he was too late. Joe Wehner was hit and killed. Luke was stunned. He roared into the swirling German planes and shot two of them down. The rest fled. On his way home he attacked a German observation plane and shot it down too. In ten minutes he had destroyed two balloons and three airplanes, but he was a different man when he landed. Wehner was gone and Luke knew he would never forget him.

Now Frank Luke began a private war with Germany. He found a new partner and set out to destroy the whole German air force. When this second partner was killed he decided to go it alone. More experienced pilots like Eddie Rickenbacker tried to slow him down, to teach him to be more careful, but Luke wouldn't listen.

One evening The Arizona Balloon Buster took off alone to hunt for his favorite prey. An hour later several men of Frank Luke's squadron, along with Eddie Rickenbacker, stood on the flying field in the growing darkness waiting for the sound of his Spad's engine. It never came.

Later they learned what had happened. After downing three more balloons in his fearless way he was attacked from the air. In the dogfight that followed he shot down two more planes. (That made eighteen victories in the fantastically short time of seventeen days.) Then he was hit himself. But he wouldn't give up. Wounded, Luke managed to land his Spad near a stream. He drew his pistol and began firing at the ground troops coming toward him. A moment later he fell dead from a rifle bullet.

In World War I only two American aces were awarded our country's highest decoration, the Congressional Medal of Honor. Frank Luke was one of them. The other was Edward V. Rickenbacker.

During the few months Rickenbacker actually flew at the front he scored the impressive total of twenty-six victories, making him America's top ace. Given the time and the opportunity he certainly could have matched the higher scores of many European pilots. And yet Eddie Rickenbacker might not have been given the chance to fight at all if it hadn't been for Billy Mitchell.

Rickenbacker was one of our greatest race-car drivers. When war came he enlisted immediately and was taught to fly. But the Army thought his mechanical abilities would be of more use on the ground and he was assigned to a flying field in France to deal with aircraft engineering problems. Then he was ordered to be General Pershing's personal driver. One day he was driving the General's car behind Billy Mitchell's powerful Mercedes when Mitchell's car broke down. Rickenbacker was the only person there who could fix it. Mitchell remembered him and the next time Eddie requested a transfer to the front it was granted.

Rickenbacker was almost the opposite of Frank Luke. Eddie was an excellent flier, while only Frank's sheer reckless courage made up for his sloppy technique. Rickenbacker was a team man, who watched over the other members of his squadron; Luke was a "loner" who wanted nothing to do with most of his fellow fliers.

In almost no time at all Rick was made a flight commander in the 94th Squadron. The superior leadership of a flier like Rickenbacker was desperately needed. The Germans were flying a new Fokker plane, the famous D-VII, and the outdated Nieuports the 94th was using just couldn't stand up to them. Even the veteran Raoul Lufbery, who had taught Rickenbacker most of what he knew, had been shot down. But Rickenbacker felt that superior skill could still beat the Germans, and he set out to prove it. Once he returned from a dogfight to discover three bullet holes just behind his cockpit. He ordered Maltese crosses painted over the holes to remind him to keep looking in every direction while on patrol. He never forgot again.

He also began to wonder why his machine guns would jam every once in a while, often at just the wrong moment. He figured out that usually a defective cartridge did it, and thereafter he spent hours checking the bullets which went into his ammunition drum.

In September, 1918, Captain Edward Rickenbacker was made Commanding Officer of the whole 94th Squadron. The first thing he did was to call all the mechanics together and tell them that he didn't want to see any more planes in the 94th listed as "unavail-

Captain Edward Rickenbacker in his Nieuport fighter getting ready for patrol.

able"—meaning unfit for duty. He talked to the Army mechanics the way he used to talk to his own mechanics in his racing days and they respected him. Next he called all the pilots together and told them that the 94th was no longer going to take a back seat to the relatively new 27th (in which Frank Luke flew).

Then he took off all alone and shot down two German planes. The men who flew the "Hat-in-the-Ring" felt a growing excitement. Just a short while back they had finally been given the new French Spad plane and now they had a new leader who meant business. In less than a week the 94th passed the 27th in total victories and no other squadron ever caught up with them.

Captain Rickenbacker had shown conclusively that the "Top Brass" had made no mistake in making him commanding officer over dozens of officers of higher rank and longer service. More than that, Rick was proving to be the best fighter pilot among them all. Although he often "gave" victories to younger pilots by letting them step in after he had set up the "kill," he still managed to outfly and outshoot every other pilot in the whole First Pursuit Group. By October he had shot down twelve of the new German Fokker D-VIIs as well as several Albatrosses and observation ships. On top of this he had attacked and sent flaming to earth five German balloons.

As the dogfights continued more deadly than ever over No Man's Land, Billy Mitchell at last found the opportunity to give airpower a chance to show what it could do in combined operations. On September 13, 1918, the great offensive at St. Mihiel began. America threw half a million troops against the Germans who were strongly entrenched in the shape of a giant "V". The Americans had the Germans hemmed inside the V; however, they could either escape or be supplied through the open end.

Billy Mitchell had a plan. He decided to use every plane in his command against the St. Mihiel sector. He assembled almost 1,500 planes and sent them against the Germans, first hitting one side of the V and then the other. The German pilots could not defend against such a ferocious and perfectly organized attack. Mitchell's bombers were free to hit the supply and reinforcement areas with 127 tons of bombs.

In two days 16,000 Germans surrendered, and St.

Mihiel fell. Colonel Billy Mitchell was promoted to General.

Early in October intelligence reports indicated that the Germans were themselves building up for another strong attack in the Meuse-Argonne Line. On the 9th Mitchell sent almost 500 fighters and bombers into the area. The fighters broke through stiff defense patrols and the bombers let loose over thirty tons of high explosives on the German reinforcements, so demoralizing the troops that the attack was not made. Our losses were not light, but airpower had shown its first worth. "It was indeed," General Mitchell wrote, "the dawn of the day when great air forces will be capable of definitely affecting a ground decision on the field of battle."

On November 11, 1918, the First World War came to an end with victory for the Allies. Millions of men had been engaged in a deadly struggle for four long years. The American air force was still relatively small at the War's end, but it had made itself felt. It had destroyed 781 enemy planes and 73 balloons, while losing only 289 planes and 48 balloons.

1921-1925

Billy Mitchell Bombs the Battleships

In a sense, the war was over too soon for Billy Mitchell. He had only begun to demonstrate the role he thought airpower should play in the affairs of the world.

He returned from Europe more flamboyant than ever. He wore a tunic with outsized patch pockets,

pink breeches (which soon became famous), and
often carried a gold-headed cane. For Mitchell was
more than a prophet, he was a showman—but a
showman with a cause. Military men and reporters
from all over the world came to see him and listen
to his ideas.

But not all listened in agreement. This "upstart"
flier, as some called him, was attacking the very basis
of traditional military thinking. In particular the
Navy was up in arms. How could anyone dare state
that the Navy was no longer capable of defending
our shores? And who could possibly believe a man
who said that a battleship, the most destructive and
indestructible machine of modern war, was now at
the mercy of the airplane? Such opinions implied
that the Air Service was important enough to be a
separate and independent member of our armed
forces, equal to the Army and Navy!

But Billy Mitchell was more than a talker. He was
a doer. In July, 1921, he found the chance he was
looking for. According to treaty, several German
warships had to be destroyed after the war. Mitchell
asked—indeed, demanded—that he be allowed to

show what his bombers could do against the condemned German ships.

Perhaps if he had not been so successful in getting
his ideas before the public, his request would not have
been granted. There was another factor, too. President Harding liked the way Billy did things. He was
told to go ahead.

The Navy was furious. Sinking battleships was its
province. Besides, it would just be a waste of time.
The former Secretary of the Navy, Josephus Daniels,
offered to stand on the bridge of the German dreadnaught *Ostfriesland* during the attack, so disdainful
was he of the accuracy of the 600-pound bombs
Mitchell's planes were to carry.

As it turned out it was a good thing former Secretary Daniels stayed aboard the U.S.S. *Henderson*
with the rest of the official observers. Mitchell had
trained his pilots well. On July 13th he led them
over the German destroyer *G-102,* which was an-
chored off Chesapeake Bay, and sent it quickly to
the bottom. Five days later six Army bombers attacked the cruiser *Frankfurt.* In eleven minutes it
joined the *G-102* fifty fathoms below. Billy Mitchell,

an identifying streamer fixed to his plane, swooped low over the shaken observers on the *Henderson*. He came so close they could see him grinning at them.

The mammoth 27,000-ton battleship *Ostfriesland* was next on the schedule, and there was no doubt in anyone's mind that she represented the real test. The *Ostfriesland* had already proved herself almost indestructible. In the Battle of Jutland she had withstood eighteen direct hits from giant 12- and 14-inch guns; later she had struck a mine. But her triple hull and dozens of water-tight compartments had saved her, and without any doubt would continue to save her—or so the Navy insisted.

The first attack on the evening of July 20th seemed to indicate that maybe Mitchell had met his match. The 600-pound bombs fell all around the *Ostfriesland* but with little serious damage. Mitchell, however, had foreseen that he could not hope to destroy such a dreadnaught with ordinary bombs. Secretly he had ordered his Martin MB-2 bombers fitted with giant blockbusters, each weighing an incredible 2,000 pounds! They were the largest ever made. Ordinarily the TNT poured into such a bomb would take ten days to cool, but by then the tests would be over. Luckily, someone thought of packing the bombs in ice. It worked and they were delivered to Mitchell just in time.

The next day the officials on the *Henderson* watched skeptically as Mitchell's bombers, which looked like small specks against the sky, circled overhead and then formed a line pointed directly toward their target.

"There he is!" someone yelled, pointing upward. "The pennant. Look there!" High overhead they made out a smaller plane. Billy Mitchell was directing the attack personally.

Suddenly a small bomb exploded near the *Ostfriesland*. A few of the observers laughed—until they were told it was only a ranging shot.

Then there was an almost audible gasp of wonderment from the watchers. From the second Martin bomber a gigantic cigar-like object had been released. It fell, tumbling end over end, and hit near the *Ostfriesland*. A great geyser of billowing smoke and water completely covered the battleship. Those aboard the *Henderson* were shaken by the concussion from the tremendous explosion.

One after the other, at intervals of two minutes, the remaining MB-2s dropped their earth-shaking cargoes.

When the smoke and falling water cleared away the *Ostfriesland* was still there, though it was difficult to tell her condition. A few cheers went up from the *Henderson*. Mitchell had failed. The Navy still ruled the seas!

Then it was noticed that the battleship was listing to one side. Slowly, almost imperceptibly, the *Ostfriesland* was settling into the water! As her bow came up, great gaping holes showed under the waterline. Mitchell's tactics had proven correct: he had directed his men to drop the new bombs not *on* but *near* the great ship so that they would explode under water and cave in her sides.

Twenty-one minutes after the first bomb fell, the *Ostfriesland* rolled completely over and disappeared beneath the surface.

Again, in 1923, Billy Mitchell's bombers showed that they were more than a match for any battleship. Off Cape Hatteras they sank the U.S.S. *Virginia* and *New Jersey,* which had been condemned as obsolete.

The bombing was done from the unheard-of height of 10,000 feet.

All this should have been enough to substantiate Mitchell's claims for airpower. But as Admiral Sims, who agreed with Billy, put it, "The average man suffers severely from the pain of a new idea." Apparently it would take more than "proof" to convince the die-hards. Those in power still did not agree. Moreover they were beginning to resent Mitchell's popularity and his unorthodox methods of doing things.

In 1925 Billy Mitchell was demoted to his permanent rank as colonel and sent to Texas. This got him out of the way—or at least out of sight—but it couldn't keep him quiet. His voice was heard again later that same year when the Navy dirigible *Shenandoah* broke up and crashed in three parts over Ohio. Fifteen men were killed.

The tragedy of the *Shenandoah* was the culmination of a series of fatal accidents in the air. To fliers of both services, and especially to Mitchell, it represented inexcusable neglect and mismanagement. Immediately he issued a blistering public statement

General "Billy" Mitchell boldly demonstrated his belief in airpower by destroying (*below*) the "unsinkable" German battleship *Ostfriesland*.

which accused the high commands of both the Army and Navy of "incompetency, criminal negligence, and almost treasonable administration of the National Defense."

Of course such insubordination could not be overlooked. Mitchell was court-martialed. But his trial brought the state of our military defenses to the attention of everyone in the country. And even though he was found guilty and suspended from the Air Service, Billy Mitchell always felt that what he had done was worth it.

Since he could not stand inactivity he resigned from the Army in order to continue his fight for airpower.

Ten years later he died. But his independent spirit, his belief in the important future of airpower, never died. Men who knew him then and men who read about him later were inspired by his memory. And such an inspiration was needed, for in the 1920s there was a great deal left to do.

1919-1929

The Golden Age

Between 1920 and 1921 there were more than 330 serious crashes in the Air Service. Nearly seventy men were killed and almost thirty badly injured. Since there were less than 1,000 pilots and observers in the Army at this time, this meant that every year one out of every ten could expect to be killed or hurt. These crashes weren't the fault of the men. They were almost inevitable in the old planes left over from World War I.

Yet the decade after the Great War has been called "the golden age of aviation," and by no less an authority than General Arnold himself. For in spite of the almost insurmountable obstacles of obsolete equipment and official apathy, Army pilots made daring flights and set record after record.

As far as the Air Service fliers of the Twenties were concerned, there were no limitations; there were only new problems to be worked out, new chances to be taken. They were a breed apart, truly pioneers of a new age. Many of their achievements may not seem startling to us today, but certainly they were not commonplace then. With each new success the public's interest grew. Newspapers discovered that these flights made "good copy" and so they often featured them.

Few Americans, for instance, had ever seen a bomber until 1919 when Colonel Hartz and Lieutenant Harmon took their Martin MB-2 on a nearly 10,000-mile flight around the borders of the United

States. They were in the air a total of 114 hours and 25 minutes.

In 1921, Hap Arnold got himself into a cross-country race with a pigeon. He almost lost when he couldn't get his motor started for forty-five minutes. Of more importance was the altitude record Lieutenant John Macready set in September of that year. Suffering from extreme cold in an exposed cockpit and kept alive only by an oxygen tube stuck in his mouth, he managed to take his LePere biplane to an astonishing height of 34,508 feet.

The first "air-to-air" refueling was made in July of the same year when Wesley May, with a five-gallon can of gasoline strapped to his back, leaped in mid air from the wing of one plane to another. In August of 1923 Lieutenants Smith and Richter stayed aloft for over thirty-seven hours by refueling their old DH-4 bomber with a fifty-foot hose from a sister plane.

Again in 1923 came the first nonstop coast-to-coast flight. It was the idea of Lieutenant Oakley Kelley, and he talked Macready into going along with him. Their first two attempts failed—once when they were more than halfway across. The third flight almost failed too when they got lost for several hours in the Arizona mountains, but at last they made it to San Diego. Upon landing Kelley offered his partner a drink from the thermos jug. "Well what do you know," said Macready. "The coffee's still hot." They had been flying almost twenty-seven hours.

Exciting as these accomplishments were, nothing cheered Americans so much as the round-the-world flight which our Air Service fliers began in April of 1924. Many other countries, including England and France, had tried it and failed. Our preparations were extensive. Four new planes were built by Douglas for the flight; agreements were made with twenty-two countries for landing fields around the world. In September, 175 days later, two of the Douglas World Cruisers returned to their starting point, Seattle, Washington. The other two had crashed, one into an Alaskan mountainside, but no one was killed.

That same year Lieutenant Russell Maughan decided that his new Curtiss PW-8 pursuit plane could make a dawn-to-dusk flight from New York to San Francisco. Three times he was forced to quit, although once he got as far as Wyoming. On June 23, Maughan took off again from Mitchell Field just as the sun came up. Twenty-one hours and forty-eight minutes later he landed his stubby Curtiss plane at San Francisco in time to see the last sliver of the setting sun. As he was being hauled bodily out of his ship by enthusiastic comrades, he handed a copy of the New York *Times* to the mayor of San Francisco. For the first time an east coast newspaper was delivered to the west coast the same day it was printed.

In 1927 Charles A. Lindbergh made his famous "impossible" solo flight across the Atlantic Ocean to Paris, France, in the *Spirit of St. Louis*. And just two years later Major Carl Spaatz and Captain Ira Eaker broke all existing endurance records by keeping their Fokker tri-motor transport in the air a full week. Perhaps no other feat so startled the aviation world as did this flight of the *Question Mark*. Forty-three aerial contacts were necessary to keep the plane aloft; almost 6,000 gallons of gasoline were transferred to the *Question Mark* as well as oil, batteries and food. Altogether the plane flew 11,000 miles during its spectacular 160-hour marathon.

The airplane had proved itself. No longer could anyone consider it an unimportant toy or only a minor part of our military forces. The American pilot had proved himself, too. He was more aggressive, more imaginative, and more skilled than any other in the world. It was really the lonely man in the cockpit who had made all the records, and his daring and his belief in airpower made him unbeatable.

There were hundreds of great fliers in the Twenties, but perhaps none of them was more outstanding than a young second lieutenant by the name of James Doolittle.

Colonel Hap Arnold first heard of Jimmy Doolittle when he had to reprimand him for "bad conduct." Doolittle had bet a friend he could sit on the landing gear of a plane while it landed. After the plane took off Doolittle climbed out of the cockpit and down to the landing gear and sat on the cross bar. Finally the pilot had to land. Doolittle won his bet, but Arnold had to ground him for a month. Secretly the Colonel felt that Jimmy Doolittle would either become a useless show-off or a great flier.

As it turned out he became a great flier, one of the greatest ever born in this country. He was always experimenting, always trying something new. For a while he was called a "Chinese Ace," which meant that he was apt to crack up any plane he flew; but that was because he always wanted to do more than the plane could. By 1921 he was chosen as one of the pilots Billy Mitchell gathered at Langley Field to perfect new bombing techniques, and so Doolittle became part of the dedicated team that sank the *Ostfriesland*. A year later, he made the first transcontinental crossing in a single day. To save weight he stripped every excess part from a DH-4 biplane. The flight began at Pablo Beach, Florida, and almost immediately he ran into a severe thunder and lightning storm. But he made it to Kelley Field, Texas, where he refueled and took off again immediately for San Diego. The flight lasted twenty-one hours and nineteen minutes. And Jimmy Doolittle became a national hero.

But Doolittle was more than an outstanding pilot. He was a student, too. He wanted to know the answers to dozens of engineering problems basic to flight. There was an engineering school at McCook Field in Ohio and Jimmy enrolled there in 1922. For the first time he had the opportunity to study an airplane from prop to rudder as a scientist.

A year later the Air Service began making plans for its round-the-world flight. This was the sort of challenge Jimmy Doolittle loved. There was a more important challenge offered him, however. The Air Service had many good pilots, not as outstanding perhaps as Jimmy, but more than equal to the world trip. What the future Air Force really needed were pilot-engineers. His superiors wanted to send Doolittle to the most exacting school of engineering in the United States, the Massachusetts Institute of Technology.

Doolittle went, and several years later at the age of twenty-eight he became one of the few men in the country with a doctor's degree in aeronautical engineering. More important, he was now ready to attack the unknown.

One of the first things he wanted to find out was how much a pursuit plane could stand, and how much the man in it could stand. The Army was considering a new plane and Jimmy was asked to test it. He took it through every maneuver he knew—loops at high speeds, rolls, spirals, tailspins, and power dives from 18,000 feet. Once when he landed he found that the wings of the plane had almost been pulled off. He was pleased; now he knew exactly how much the little ship would take.

Racing, of course, appealed to him tremendously. In 1925 the Army had won the Pulitzer race against the Navy in a Curtiss plane. Doolittle decided to fit pontoons to the fast little racer and enter the international Schneider Cup Race for seaplanes. England had won it twice and so had Italy, but they had never been up against a pilot like Doolittle. Instead of making the usual wide turn around each pylon, Jimmy dived at the mark from above, making a tight vertical bank around it. The established speed record for the race was 177 miles per hour. Doolittle streaked around the course at a speed of 232.57 miles per hour and took the cup home for America.

Now that his name was known the world over,

Lieutenant Jimmy Doolittle stands on the pontoon of his Curtiss Racer after winning the Schneider Cup Race in 1925.

Jimmy Doolittle became our top exhibition pilot. He even demonstrated the Curtiss fighter in South America. On one of his trips down there he broke both ankles in an accident just before the flight. But he wanted to go on with the exhibition anyway. He asked to be strapped in the plane, his feet tied to the rudder bar; in extreme pain he showed off the Curtiss plane to amazed spectators. On this same flight he even beat a famous German World War I ace, who was showing off his own country's planes, in a mock dogfight.

His ankles were so badly broken he had to remain in bed for six months after that flight. But his mind was working out new ideas and plans. Was it possible, he wondered, to do an *outside* loop? An ordinary "loop-the-loop" was easy; as the plane pulled up and over, the pilot was forced safely down into the cockpit by the centrifugal force of the loop. During an outside loop, however, the pilot would begin by pushing the stick forward, keeping it there while the plane went into a dive and then tucked under on its back and finally—he hoped—pulled out of the unnatural maneuver. Furthermore an outside loop would tend to throw the pilot out of the plane; and even if the seat belt held him in, wouldn't the strong centrifugal force injure his vital organs or perhaps even kill him?

By the time Doolittle left the hospital he had determined that his Curtiss plane could execute an outside loop without damage—but he still didn't know if a pilot could.

In the summer of 1927 he decided to try it. With

an extra-strong safety belt drawn tightly about his waist, he took his fighter to 10,000 feet and put it into a screaming dive. Then with both hands he continued to push the stick forward. The blood rushed to his head. He felt his body straining outward against the belt with a force of 450 pounds as the stubby Curtiss plane began to come out of the screaming dive—on its back. Stubbornly he shoved with all his strength against the stick. Slowly the plane began to pull up, its wing wires taut with the strain, and then it came out on top of the loop. He had made it! Afterwards he made light of the feat, telling reporters he had done it on the spur of the moment; only his close friends knew of the lengthy study and preparation he had made before the actual attempt.

Being the first man to fly an outside loop was a startling accomplishment, but to Doolittle not a very important one. He was more interested in the major problems that were still unsolved. In his doctor's thesis at MIT he had shown that even the most experienced pilot couldn't tell how level his plane was or even which way the wind was blowing unless he could see what was around him. "Blind flying" then was a major hazard, and certainly landing a plane when the visibility was zero seemed impossible. But was it? Jimmy Doolittle didn't think it was.

For several years the Guggenheim Fund for the Promotion of Aeronautics had been financing a world-wide organization which was looking into such problems. In 1928 the Army put Doolittle in charge of its experiments in blind flying. He lost no time in going to work.

First of all, he knew he wanted flying instruments that would be more accurate than any made before. He even needed instruments that hadn't been thought of before. His plan was to seek out the direction to an airport by means of radio beams. Another beam would tell him when he had crossed the edge of the field. But then he needed to know exactly how high he was and how accurate he was in making his turns so that he could fly through the landing pattern and come down safely without once seeing the ground.

In 1928 there wasn't such a thing as a true altimeter. It had to be designed, and it had to be finer than any watch. A magnetic compass couldn't be used; it was too unreliable for such work. A compass using a gyroscopic principle was needed. Help came from everywhere. Soon the research departments of many of the top instrument companies in America were at work on the project.

By September, 1929, the plane was ready. Everything had been tested as thoroughly as possible, except under the actual condition of "blind flight." On the morning of the 24th Doolittle climbed into his plane and made a final check of his new instruments: the complex radio equipment which could pick up two types of beacons, the sensitive Kollsman barometric altimeter, the Sperry artificial horizon and directional gyroscope.

Then a hood was pulled over his cockpit so he couldn't see anything outside the plane. He heard someone say, "Good luck, Jim." He knew that a friend, Ben Kelsey, was riding in the front cockpit in case something went wrong, but still . . .

As the biplane roared down the field, Doolittle kept his eyes glued to the instrument panel. Then he felt the little plane lift from the ground. The directional gyro was vertical, the artificial horizon level. So far so good.

He flew west for five miles, turned and flew back across the field. From the ground the anxious watchers could see Ben Kelsey's arms resting outside the cockpit. Doolittle made a perfect 180-degree turn again. Now he could pick out the correct approach beam on his special radio. He began to nose down, watching the needle of the sensitive Kollsman altimeter. When he saw he was a few feet above the field, according to his instruments, he eased back on the stick. Was he too soon, or too late? There was a slight bump, and then he could feel the plane rolling smoothly along the ground. Someone pulled back the canvas hood and Doolittle, blinking, looked around. He had landed only a few feet from his take-off point!

The next morning the New York *Times* carried a front-page story about the flight:

BLIND PLANE FLIES 15 MILES AND
LANDS; FOG PERIL OVERCOME

It was a fitting climax to the "Golden Age."

1930-1940

The Birth of a Queen

On August 8, 1934, the United States Army Air Corps sent out a circular from Wright Field to all major aircraft companies. The Air Corps wanted a new "multi-engined" bomber. It had to be able to deliver 2,000 pounds of bombs; it had to fly at least 200 miles per hour, but 250 was really wanted; it had to have a range of over 2,000 miles, and carry a crew of from four to six men.

Claire Egtvedt of the Boeing Airplane Company read the circular and began thinking. For many years Boeing had built speedy little biplane fighters which had been particularly successful in both services. But for some time Egtvedt had thought that Boeing should enter the large plane field with transports and bombers. Slowly commercial aviation was giving larger and larger orders to aircraft manufacturers and there was a growing dissatisfaction in the military over the quality and performance of its bombers.

The small, speedy fighter plane obviously had its uses and easily engaged the imagination of the public, but the top men in the Air Corps knew that a bomber that could fly high enough and fast enough and far enough was America's best defense in the air. For a long time, however, the bomber was merely an oversized biplane. It was slow, it could carry only a few bombs, and its range was severely limited.

Never had the sad state of military aviation been brought so dramatically to the attention of the public as it had earlier that same year when the Air Corps was asked to fly the mail. The winter of 1934 was one of the worst in modern history. The planes the Air Corps fliers had to use were obsolete bombers and sometimes open-cockpit fighters with limited instruments. The results were scandalous and tragic. Fourteen good pilots lost their lives before the fiasco was called off.

To the public this sad showing meant only that the Army had fallen down on the job, that it couldn't even keep up with the ordinary commercial flying of the day. But there was more to it than that. The Air Corps fliers had no training for such work; their aircraft were not equipped to fly at night and in such weather.

Still, there was a lot of truth in the accusations. The Army's planes *were* falling behind in performance. Many an Air Corps flier had returned to his base angry and embarrassed after being passed in the air by a commercial air liner.

Why couldn't the Army do something about this? Well, with the aid of men like Claire Egtvedt, and airplane companies like Boeing, it was attempting to do so. Back in 1928 Boeing had designed a sleek, all-metal, low-wing monoplane called the *Monomail*. It was far ahead of its time—so far, in fact, that it needed a variable-pitch propeller for top performance and such a device had not yet been developed. But from the *Monomail* idea came a new design for a bomber. It was a twin-engined, high-speed monoplane with retractable landing gear and a long monocoque fuselage. The Army called it the B-9.

Other aircraft manufacturers were at work on new designs too, however, and just as Boeing brought out the B-9, the Martin company introduced another bomber. It was named the B-10.

The Martin B-10 was really the first of our modern bombers. It was an all-metal, mid-wing airplane, with retractable landing gear and a power nose turret. The crew were completely enclosed. Out of six designs submitted to the Air Corps in 1932 the Martin bomber clearly outclassed them all. It had a top speed of 207 m.p.h. and a ceiling of over 20,-000 feet. Even the fastest pursuit plane could hardly catch it.

Certainly it had Boeing's entry, the B-9, out-classed. . . .

Egtvedt studied the new circular again. "Multi-engined," it said. Usually that meant two engines, but he wondered. Perhaps four engines were needed. He took the next plane from Boeing's plant in Seattle and flew to Wright Field to see Major Howard, the engineering chief. Would the Army consider a four-engine bomber in the competition? Major Howard saw no objection.

Egtvedt flew back to Seattle and called his staff together. He knew they were taking a big chance. The B-9 had failed. A commercial air liner the company had produced had not drawn the orders it should have. Perhaps more important, America was in the throes of the worst depression in its history. It was going to be difficult enough, if not impossible, to design and build a giant four-engined bomber in a year; if it failed the company would be ruined. Boeing decided to go ahead anyway.

To build a giant four-engined bomber within a year required the services of every man in the company and almost all of the money available for this and other projects as well. First, three-view plans were drawn up. They presented a beautiful monoplane with wings over one hundred feet from tip to tip and a body eighty-eight feet long. A small model was built and given one hundred hours of tests in a wind tunnel. The results were exciting. Not only did it look as if the four 700-horsepower Hornet engines would give it the required top speed, but the indications were that the range might be as good as 3,000 miles. The plane was designated the 299.

There were thousands of problems to be solved, however: should flaps be used, or shouldn't they? How could the landing gear fold into the same place which already held two of the engines? Where could the company get more money? (The original estimate was $150,000 short.)

But the men of Boeing solved every problem and just nine months after the decision to go ahead was given the giant plane was completed and shipped to Boeing field under secret wraps. On July 28, 1935, the 299 was rolled from its hangar for its first trials. Five machine-gun turrets bristled from its body. It even had a seat for a person called a "co-pilot." Newspaper reporters were amazed at the sight. It was like a huge battleship of the sky. One writer called it a veritable *flying fortress*. The name stuck.

The great plane flew beautifully. On its way to the military tests (its first cross-country flight) it averaged an incredible 235 m.p.h., and arrived nonstop at Dayton, Ohio, two hours before the Army expected it. There were several other bombers in the competition, all of them conventional two-engined types. They were good planes, but all eyes were on the "Flying Fortress."

The tests began. The bombers were to be checked for speed, altitude, range, power, climb, armament, ease of maintenance, landing characteristics, weight-lifting—the list was a long one.

Very soon it was evident to everyone that the 299 was way ahead of the field. Then tragedy struck. On a routine take-off the 299 seemed to be climbing too steeply. Suddenly it stalled and dived toward the ground. It began to pull out, but not quickly enough. There was a tremendous explosion and a mountain of smoke and flame arose from the crash as the wing tanks ignited. Three men managed to get out alive. Two were killed.

What had happened? It was discovered that the 299 had taken off with its tail surfaces still locked. This plane was so big that some of its controls had to be locked while it was on the ground to protect them against strong gusts of wind. The very complexity of this "flying fortress" had helped destroy it.

There was no way to win the contest now, but men like Hap Arnold were so impressed by what they had seen that they insisted that Boeing be given the go-ahead to build thirteen of the four-engined ships, even though the Air Corps had to award the main contract to another company. The Boeing plane was to be called the B-17.

Boeing's far-sighted gamble had paid off. Thirteen airplanes weren't much of a beginning, but as the 1930s drew to a close it became more and more evident that the B-17 Flying Fortress was a plane America needed desperately. Other companies tried to best it—notably the Consolidated with their B-24 "Liberator"—but none really could. It was a design capable of infinite improvement to meet the growing

One of the first Boeing B-17s, flying at an altitude of 13,000 ft.

demands of modern war.

Boeing was asked immediately to build an even bigger airplane, a superbomber. Years later, at the height of World War II, it would be known the world over as the mighty B-29 "Superfortress."

The story of the Flying Fortress has been emphasized here not only because it is typical of American daring and foresight in aviation, but because the B-17 was more than just a big airplane. It was the first representative of a new kind of bomber which was the embodiment of Billy Mitchell's concept of airpower.

America did not have a large air fleet as the crucial decade of the 1940s began. In fact, the number of up-to-date aircraft on hand at the time was shockingly small. Yet it is important to remember that so well had Air Corps planners looked ahead and so well had America's designers met the challenges given them, that all of the combat airplanes flown by Air Force pilots in World War II were designed before that war began.

1941-1942

Pearl Harbor, Bataan— and the *Hornet's* Sting

Several unusual and ominous events occurred early in the morning on December 7, 1941, near our naval base at Pearl Harbor, Hawaii. Just before seven o'clock a midget Japanese submarine was sunk as it crept close to the harbor. A few minutes later the aircraft carrier *Enterprise* heard a frantic plea from one of its pilots on patrol: "Don't shoot. I'm American!" He was being shot down by Japanese Zeros.

No one in command paid any more attention to these "warnings" than to the direct report sent in by Technician 3rd Class Joe Lockard. Lockard was in charge of one of the six experimental radar sets on the island. So many things had gone wrong with these sets that Headquarters had decided they were only to be used a few hours every morning. Neither Joe Lockard nor his assistant, Private George Elliott, had ever seen a "blip," indicating aircraft, on the radar screen.

A little after seven o'clock Lockard suddenly called out, "Hey, George! Come here! Look!"

There on the screen a giant blip was moving southward. Joe and his assistant plotted its course. They figured that the planes the blip represented were going about 225 m.p.h. and were headed straight for Pearl Harbor.

Lockard excitedly called Central Control and reported the formation of planes. The officer he talked to didn't seem very impressed. "Okay," he said, "I've got it. Don't worry."

Nothing was done about the report. A flight of B-17s was due in from the States. That was all that could be out there.

Approximately one hour later the first wave of Japanese planes attacked Pearl Harbor, and the first bomb fell on the majestic battleship *Arizona*. Two hours later it was all over. Of the eight battleships in the harbor, five were sunk. One hundred and forty-one planes of the Army Air Corps were destroyed and more than that number of Navy aircraft. In one mighty blow from the air, the Japanese had put out of commission—much of it permanently—seventy-five per cent of America's total military force in the Pacific. Because the attack was a total surprise, the enemy lost only twenty-nine airplanes.

When the attack first began Lieutenants George Welch and Ken Taylor were trying to decide whether or not to take a swim.

As machine gun bullets spattered all around them they ran to the Officers' Club and Welch called Haleiwa Field, on the northern tip of the island.

"Get two P-40s ready for Taylor and me!" he

The Japanese surprise attack on Pearl Harbor brought destruction to airplanes parked on airfields and battleships docked in the harbor.

yelled. "It's not a gag. The Japs are here!"

They reached Haleiwa in a record ten minutes and climbed into their planes. They found a squadron of dive bombers circling over Ewa, a Marine air base. Side by side Welch and Taylor attacked. They both shot down two Japanese planes.

Only seven United States fighter planes managed to get into the air that day, but they shot down twelve enemy planes. George Welch got four of them himself (he took off three times). Hap Arnold recommended him for the Congressional Medal of Honor, but it was never acted upon because Welch's commanding Air Officer said he had taken off without orders!

Almost all the valuable B-17s were destroyed while parked on the fields around Pearl Harbor.

The same thing happened on December 8th at Clark Field several thousand miles to the west in the Philippines. All but two or three of the nineteen Flying Fortresses at Clark were caught on the ground and destroyed. Counting the two squadrons at Mindanao to the south, this left a bombing force of less than twenty B-17s to go it alone against Japan.

The next day Major Emmett "Rosy" O'Donnell flew up from Mindanao to Clark Field to check conditions before bringing on the rest of his squadron. He was shocked at the wreckage and destruction. No sooner had he arrived than there was an air raid warning. He took off immediately with two other B-17s. At least in the air they had a chance.

They had left the field to escape the pending attack, but they were on their first bombing mission too. An invasion fleet was reported approaching the coast of Luzon. The three Flying Forts were ordered to fan out and search the area. At 25,000 feet Rosy O'Donnell spotted a large ship. It looked like a carrier. Every man in the plane wanted to be a part of the crew that sank that first ship. Unfortunately the bomb release jammed. Flying through dangerous flak, it took forty-five minutes to drop all the bombs. None of them hit the zigzagging ship.

One of the other B-17s had better luck. It was piloted by Colin Kelly. He spotted what he thought was a battleship near the coast. His bombardier sent a string of six-hundred-pound bombs toward the ship. One scored a direct hit!

Then Japanese fighters came up after Kelly. He and his men fought off two—then six more roared in. A shell hit the navigator's compartment. A waist gunner fell dead.

"Give 'em all you've got," Kelly cried. "Beat 'em off!"

Then the left wing caught fire and the elevator cables were cut. Kelly yelled for his crew to bail out. They did. But Colin Kelly's body was found near his wrecked Fortress.

He had sunk the first enemy ship. And he was our first national hero of World War II.

By nightfall of December 10th, the fighter-plane strength of the whole Philippines was reduced to twenty operational Curtiss P-40s and a few P-35s. Earlier that day thirty-five American P-40s and P-35s took off to intercept an attacking force of two hundred Japanese planes. Only five Americans returned, all with badly damaged planes.

On December 24th, General MacArthur decided

that since his troops no longer had adequate air protection he would have to concentrate his forces on Bataan peninsula. Then he sent eight of the remaining P-40s to Mindanao. That left only a few fighters under Colonel Harold H. George, the Chief of Staff of the 5th Interceptor Command (several P-40s had to be dismantled for their parts), against over 600 enemy planes reported in the area.

Thus began one of the most heroic episodes in the history of the Air Force.

George's men cut a landing field out of the jungle at Bataan and two other places and fortified them as best they could. To the north 20,000 Americans and Filipinos were trying desperately to hold off 100,000 Japanese troops. Then the Japanese landed 3,500 more troops and completely surrounded the Bataan peninsula. Colonel George could expect no help from the already outnumbered American Army.

Every man at the field took up arms, including cooks, fitters, and staff personnel. Supplies and ammunition were flown in to Bataan every night from Mindanao by Captain Jesus Villamor in an old 300-h.p. Bellanca passenger plane.

On Bataan life became a nightmare. The jungles were filled with Japanese. At night they tried to infiltrate the weak lines; once they even got close enough to throw two hand grenades into Colonel George's tent.

At night too our pilots tried to strafe and bomb the enemy landings in Manila Bay. Cans full of sand soaked with gasoline made an improvised outline of the field. Each take-off was as dangerous as the mission itself. The P-40s weren't intended for night flying. Furthermore, the men were wearing out along with the planes. Their vision was growing poor from lack of proper food. In two nights three P-40s crashed into the trees; two pilots were killed immediately—the third, suffering horribly from burns, jumped to his death from Captain Villamor's Bellanca as he was being flown to Mindanoa for treatment.

By January 26th the Japanese had established two central airfields of their own in the Philippines. General George decided to attack them. His pilots were in no condition to fly by now (they were underweight by an average of forty pounds) but seven were picked. Boyd "Buzz" Wagner, already an ace, was to be their leader.

The take-off was especially dangerous. The Japanese were watching the field and it was impossible to water it down. The dust from the fighters taking off got so bad that it blinded the pilot of the seventh P-40, and he crashed.

But the attack was a success. At one field Buzz Wagner and his valiant men destroyed twenty-four planes; they left thirteen burning on the other. They had caught the enemy completely by surprise.

The nightmare continued. Jesus Villamor completed a spectacular photo reconnaissance mission in a slow Stearman biplane used for training. He barely got back alive. The P-40s protecting him shot down five Japanese Zeros.

Two weeks later there were only four P-40s left.

On the 3rd of March six enemy ships were reported approaching the island with thousands of troops. They were the reinforcements the Japanese were waiting for. General George knew those ships had to be stopped somehow. He had only one pilot left out of the eighty who had come with him from

Captain William Dyess, a hero of Bataan.

the States a year before—Captain William Dyess. Furthermore, there were only two bombs left. Captain Dyess' P-40 was fitted with one of these bombs and, with the slight protection of the three remaining P-40s flown by replacements, he was sent to cripple the transports.

Dyess barely made it off the field with the 500-pound bomb. Over Subic Bay he found the ships. The four fighters dived on them. Dyess' bomb fell close to the hull of the largest transport, caving in her sides. She capsized. Incendiary bullets from another P-40 exploded a tanker. The pilots of these small, single-engined planes had seemingly done the impossible—but there was more to be done yet.

Dyess returned to his field and eight men loaded on the remaining bomb. Over Subic Bay again Dyess attacked another transport. He managed a direct hit this time, though his P-40 almost came apart under the strain of the long dive.

As the four pilots began strafing the remaining ships, swift Japanese Zeros attacked them. There were almost forty of them. Lieutenants Fosse, Stinson and Crellin were shot down. Dyess continued to fight, though he was wounded five times and in his already weakened condition he kept "blacking out" every time he made a tight turn.

The battle carried Dyess back over his own base. General George saw him desperately trying to evade the Zeros and suddenly knelt down in prayer for his last pilot's life. Dyess' plane was trailing smoke. It didn't look as if he had a chance. Suddenly Dyess turned his P-40 on its back and jumped out. He waited to open his parachute until just before he hit the jungle so that the Japanese couldn't machine-gun him on the way down.

Captain Dyess, who was awarded the Medal of

Honor, was safe. But there were no P-40s left on Bataan. On April 9, 1942, the American troops remaining on the peninsula surrendered.

The fall of Bataan, no matter how heroic the fight, was one of the bitterest defeats in American history. The shock of Pearl Harbor was still fresh in everyone's mind, and morale could not have been worse as Japanese military forces swept everything before them. Then, only nine days after the surrender, the Air Force retaliated. With the coöperation of the United States Navy, it struck back at the very heart of Japan with one of the most courageous and daring flights of the war.

The brilliant idea for the flight actually originated with Captain Francis Low, one of Admiral King's aides. When Hap Arnold was told about it, he immediately thought of Colonel Jimmy Doolittle. He could make it succeed if anyone could. Arnold sent for Doolittle late in January, 1941.

"Jim," he said, "do you think we have a plane that can take off in five hundred feet with a two-thousand-pound bomb load and fly two thousand miles?"

Doolittle guessed that Arnold was talking about a carrier take-off. The idea intrigued him, but he had no idea what it all meant.

In any case, Doolittle-the-engineer had the answer for Arnold the next day: the B-25, a two-engined, twin-tail medium bomber, could do what was asked, provided it was stripped to lighten it and extra gas tanks were added. Arnold was pleased. He then told Doolittle what was up.

The plan was to transport sixteen Air Force bombers as close to Japan as possible by aircraft carrier; these planes would then take off and bomb seven major Japanese cities. After the attack the bombers would continue on to China where there was a good chance of landing at friendly airfields.

During the first week in January, Jimmy Doolittle collected the best B-25 crews in the country at Eglin Field, Florida. He told them they were going to practice quick take-offs until they could make it within five hundred feet.

Most of the pilots thought a loaded B-25 needed at least three thousand feet. "What makes you think we can do it, Colonel?" one asked.

"Because I've done it," Doolittle said.

The B-25s were stripped. The secret and heavy Norden bombsight was replaced with a twenty-cent sight which was perfectly adequate for low-level attack. There was no bottom gun turret, no liaison radio. When Doolittle was finished with them, each B-25 weighed 1,200 pounds less than it had before.

By March the men were ready—but for what they did not know. They had never been in battle before; in fact they had never even fired the guns on their planes. But Doolittle was proud and confident of his fliers. He then asked, and received permission from Hap Arnold, to lead the men he had trained on the first strike against Japan itself.

On April 1st, the aircraft carrier *Hornet* steamed out of San Francisco with an unusual cargo—sixteen bombers and eighty officers and men of the Army Air Forces.

The plan was for the *Hornet* to approach within 500 miles of Japan so that the planes could reach China after their bombing. Doolittle himself was to take off hours earlier than the others and set Tokyo afire with incendiary bombs to help guide the others.

Unfortunately the *Hornet* and her accompanying carrier, the U. S. S. *Enterprise,* were spotted by a small Japanese patrol ship while still 823 miles off the coast. Although the patrol ship was sunk immediately, it was impossible to tell whether or not the position of the two American carriers had been reported. They could not be risked. Doolittle and his men had to take off immediately.

The sea was rough, and the deck of the *Hornet* pitched dangerously. Doolittle took off first. He made it look easy and this inspired the others. Miraculously all sixteen B-25s roared off the wet deck without accident.

Five hours later Doolittle's lead plane reached the Japanese coast. It was sighted by enemy planes, but Doolittle quickly dodged into a valley and shook them off.

Suddenly Tokyo could be seen up ahead. At an altitude of fifteen hundred feet the B-25 began its bomb run on a munitions factory. A minute later two thousand pounds of high explosives fell on the heart of Japan for the first time. The flak was thick but the plane came through unharmed. Doolittle hoped the rest of his fliers would be all right.

His B-25 headed out over the China Sea. There was supposed to be a "homing" radio signal sent from an American plane flying from Chungking, but unknown to Doolittle, this plane had crashed.

It was now night over China, and with no radio signal to guide them most of the B-25s became lost. The Chinese were suspicious, even antagonistic, to the "foreign" fliers found wandering around in the dark. Doolittle himself was almost shot when he couldn't find his parachute (a farmer had stolen it) to prove he had just bailed out. Several of the group were killed. A number were captured. (One crew member, who spent thirty-six months in prison, returned to Japan after the war as a missionary.)

With so few planes involved, the raid actually caused little military damage. It gave American morale a badly needed boost, however, and it shocked and frightened the Japanese people even more than Pearl Harbor had horrified us. Its military leaders were so stunned by the implications of the flight that they decided to keep several fighter groups at home as a protection against further attacks.

1940-1943

Tigers
and
Eagles

China, where Jimmy Doolittle landed after the bombing of Tokyo, had been at war with Japan for more then ten years. In 1931 the Japanese attacked Manchuria and the following year they captured Shanghai. By 1937 they were ready to strike at the heart of the mainland.

For years the Chinese had been trying to build up an air force, but had not been successful; now the situation was desperate. On the advice of several American pilots already working with the Chinese, Madame Chiang Kai-shek, who was the National Secretary of Aviation, asked a retired American Air Corps captain to accept full command of the Chinese Air Force. This retired officer was Claire Chennault, a man who knew as much about modern fighter-plane tactics as anyone in the world. In 1935 he had written a book on the subject; it was called *The Role of Defensive Pursuit.*

Chennault arrived at Kunming Field, China, in July of 1937. He was given the rank of colonel. At Kunming there was only the skeleton of an air force. The few aircraft there were obsolete. Madame Chiang gave Chennault a new P-36 for his personal use, and he used it to great advantage. From the air he now began directing his small force of American and Chinese pilots in the tactics of aerial warfare he knew so well.

Then, early in 1941, China was given one hundred new Curtiss P-40 Tomahawks by the American people. Though still at peace with Japan, we had finally expressed in a very concrete way our sympathy for the plight of China. Now all Colonel Chennault needed was the additional pilots to fly them. With the permission of President Roosevelt, Chennault went to pilots and old friends already flying in the various military services of the United States. From the Air Forces he recruited forty pilots; from the Navy and Marines he got sixty. The pay was good ($600 a month, plus $500 for each Japanese plane shot down) but most of the men who followed Chennault were idealists as well as adventurers. They believed in the Chinese cause.

This small band of Americans flying for China was known officially as the AVG, or the American Volunteer Group. Very shortly, however, they had another and more colorful name. Chennault had the nose of each P-40 painted to resemble a tiger shark ready to strike. The Chinese in particular liked it because the tiger was their national emblem. The group quickly became known as the Flying Tigers.

Day by day now, Claire Chennault was readying his Tigers for their first real assault on the Japanese.

He taught them all he knew about the superior Japanese Zero fighter plane; more important, he taught them how the P-40 could beat it. By December 7, 1941, he had trained three top-flight squadrons which were about to surprise the Japanese as much as they had surprised us at Pearl Harbor.

After war was declared between Japan and the United States, the Japanese stepped up their war effort all over the Far East. On December 18 Kunming Field was bombed from a very high altitude. The next day ten Japanese raiders were again reported on their way. These were bombers and they were unescorted; they had no reason as yet to fear the Chinese Air Force.

Chennault sent up four Flying Tigers to intercept the bombers. He sent fifteen more to wait for the bombers as they tried to return to their base after being attacked. The plan worked perfectly. Only four enemy bombers got home safely.

Several days later six more bombers were destroyed as well as four Japanese fighter planes. Then, on Christmas Day, 1941, one hundred enemy fighters and bombers were intercepted by eighteen Tigers in their shark-nosed P-40s. In the fight that followed thirty-three Japanese planes were shot down. The Flying Tigers lost none.

In the next three months, the Tigers averaged twenty enemy planes shot down for every one of their own they lost. It was a record never equaled before or since.

The Flying Tigers were now famous the world over. In particular they had come to the attention of Colonel Robert Scott, Jr., who was "flying The Hump" over the mountains between India and China, delivering much-needed supplies in sturdy Douglas transport planes. Bob Scott had always wanted to be a fighter pilot, but he was now thirty-four years old and the Air Force had told him he was too old. Scott didn't think so, however, and during a trip to the Tigers' base at Kunming he decided to go directly to Claire Chennault with a daring proposition.

He told Chennault that he wanted a P-40 fighter plane. He would use it against the Japanese in India and Burma. He promised to take good care of it and to give it back to the Flying Tigers whenever they wanted it.

Ordinarily, of course, such a thing would have been out of the question. Not only was it against all regulations, but it was a good way for China to lose a good airplane if the flier wasn't one of the very best. But Chennault took a strong liking to Bob Scott. And after all, what did it matter *where* the enemy was being shot down, so long as he *was* being shot down? With a twinkle in his eye, Chennault said:

"Some Forties are on the way from Africa. You get the next one that comes through. Use it as long as you want."

For Bob Scott it was a dream come true. At last he was a fighter pilot.

The first thing he did when his new P-40 arrived on April 30, 1942, was to paint the shark's face of the Flying Tigers on the cowling. Then he took the plane up for a flight. It flew so beautifully that the Kittyhawk actually seemed a part of him, and when he pressed the trigger of his six fifty-caliber machine guns their tremendous power shook the whole ship. Scott felt he could shoot down any Jap he could find.

The month of May proved to be the greatest month in Bob Scott's life. He flew every day. At the end of

General Claire L. Chennault.

the month his log book showed an amazing 214 hours in the air. He used the time well. In his personal P-40 which he nicknamed "Old Exterminator" Scott began a one-man war against the Japanese using the Burma Road. He strafed them and he bombed them. He even hit their ships and river barges. Since he was making as many as five separate missions a day, he decided to impress the enemy as much as possible. After one mission he would land

and order that his propeller spinner be painted white. For the next mission he'd have it painted red, then blue. The Japanese thought a whole squadron of P-40s was attacking their vital roadways and installations.

It was during May, too, that Bob Scott flew with the Flying Tigers on several of their strikes. He learned a lot from them. In fact, when the Flying Tigers were officially made part of the United States Air Force, Robert Scott was chosen to take command of the new Fighter Group. Claire Chennault was promoted to the rank of brigadier general and put in charge of the whole Fourteenth Air Force in China.

By July 4, 1942, when the Flying Tiger outfit was officially transferred to the U. S. Air Force, its score was 299 Japanese planes destroyed in seven months. The new pilots who replaced many of the older fliers carried on in the proud tradition. Colonel Bob Scott destroyed fourteen Japanese planes himself, and he was by no means the top scorer in the China-Burma-India theater. But he would be the first to tell you that one man, and one man alone, was responsible for our great success in the air in the Far East. His name was Claire Chennault.

Half a world away, in England, another American volunteer group had already made itself equally famous in the air. They were the World War II counterparts of the Lafayette Escadrille, only this time they flew in the Royal Air Force and they were known as the Eagle Squadron.

Actually the Eagle Squadron was formed long before the Flying Tigers. On October 30, 1940, the first squadron of Americans became operational in the R.A.F. This was, of course, considerably before America entered the war, and the problem of maintaining neutrality was a ticklish one.

In the beginning the Eagle Squadron was commanded by Englishmen, but as the Americans began to establish their ability to take care of themselves —and as two more Eagle Squadrons were formed after the original one—they were allowed to command their own groups. The first American Eagle Squadron Commander was the colorful Colonel Chesley Peterson. His story speaks for hundreds of

Flying Lieutenant Chesley Peterson (*right*) and a fellow Eagle, Flying Officer Gregory Daymond, in front of a Spitfire.

American boys who were determined to fly and fight against an enemy they knew would have to be beaten sooner or later.

When he was nineteen, Chesley Peterson changed his birth certificate so that he could give his age as twenty-one and enlisted in the U. S. Army Air Corps. Amazingly enough he was "washed out" of primary flight training school at Randolph Field, Texas, because the Air Force didn't believe he could fly well enough. When he heard that an Eagle Squadron was being formed so Americans could fly in the Royal Air Force he decided to join. The only way this could be done was to go to Canada, enlist in the Canadian

Air Force and then be transferred to England.

The first time he tried it young Peterson was "arrested" by the F. B. I. in Toronto and ordered back to the United States. The neutrality law which stopped him the first time was soon removed, however, and Peterson was allowed to enlist in Canada in June, 1940. After flight training he was sent to England. There he completed his advance training in the fine English fighter, the Hawker Hurricane. The first Eagle Squadron was formed too late to help out in the heroic Battle of Britain (in which the outnumbered but valiant pilots of the R.A.F. defeated the *Luftwaffe*) but in the months that followed the Eagles destroyed seventy-four German aircraft. Chesley Peterson got five himself and was awarded the British Distinguished Flying Cross; later the King personally presented him with the Distinguished Service Order.

By the time the Eagle Squadrons were transferred officially to the American Eighth Air Force which was building up in England they were tried and tested in battle and were invaluable in training and leading their own countrymen. Peterson, for instance, became the youngest colonel in the American military forces.

For many of the Eagles September 29, 1942, was a day of 'mixed emotions. They were being sworn into the U. S. Army Air Forces and they knew they were going to miss their old friends in the R. A. F. As they came to attention for the last time in the uniform of the R. A. F., Air Chief Marshall Sir W. Sholto Douglas addressed them:

"You joined us readily and of your own free will when our need was greatest. There are those of your number who are not here today—those sons of the United States who were the first to give their lives for their country . . ."

One thing the former Eagles noticed right away: the base pay in the R. A. F. for a pilot officer had been $76 a month; a first lieutenant in the Army Air Forces received $276 a month!

Something else came to their attention too, and it worried them. They heard that the Eighth Air Force was going to try to bomb Germany by daylight. The R. A. F. had tried that and found it too costly. Well, the Americans would learn.

1942-1945

Target–
Germany

In February, 1942, Brigadier General Ira C. Eaker arrived in England. General Arnold had just appointed him our Bomber Commander in Europe. General Eaker was to establish American bomber bases for the war against Hitler.

At first the job looked impossible. We had few

men and even fewer planes. Moreover, the British didn't think much of the B-17 Flying Fortress or of the way we planned to use it. The B-17 was a high-altitude bomber. The Norden bombsight, which was the best in the world, was meant for pinpointing specific targets; naturally it had to be used in daylight. The British bombed large target areas at night; any other system, they felt, was too dangerous.

In July the first group of Flying Fortresses arrived in England along with the officer who was appointed to command the Eighth Air Force, Major General Carl Spaatz. For two months the B-17 crews trained, readying themselves for battle. Then, on August 17th, their chance came. They were told they were going to bomb the railroad yards at Rouen, France.

Ira Eaker himself rode in the first plane, *Yankee Doodle,* which was piloted by Colonel Frank Armstrong. There were twelve Fortresses altogether. Over Rouen Eaker saw harmless looking puffs of smoke around his planes. The B-17s were rocked by the explosions of German anti-aircraft fire, but none were hit. German fighter planes tried to attack the formation but escorting British Spitfires drove them off.

The raid on Rouen was a success. And no planes were lost. On Ira Eaker's desk when he returned was a message from Sir Arthur Harris, the British Air Chief Marshall: *"Yankee Doodle* certainly went to town."

There were more raids—on Abbéville, Dieppe, Amiens. . . . Then on October 9th Eaker sent 108 heavy bombers, most of them B-17s, to bomb the industrial factories at Lille. The bombers were fiercely attacked. Four of them were shot down and few of their bombs hit anywhere near the target. By the time winter set in eighteen bombers had been lost. Were daylight raids wrong? Severe criticism was mounting.

Ira Eaker had other problems too. Jimmy Doolittle had been sent to Africa to command the newly created Twelfth Air Force which was to be used in the invasion of North Africa. All of the available resources of the Army Air Forces were poured into Africa to support our ground troops against the German forces commanded by Rommel. Ira Eaker and the Eighth Air Force had to hold up their own attacks. Frustrating as this was, the crowning blow came during the conference at Casablanca where the Allied High Command met in January of 1943. Hap Arnold told Eaker that President Roosevelt had agreed with Churchill, England's Prime Minister, to use our planes for night bombing.

This was too much for Eaker. He asked to be allowed to present his viewpoint to Churchill personally. Hap Arnold agreed to the plan.

When Ira Eaker saw Churchill he told him bluntly that to use the American bombers for night bombing would be a great mistake. Then he added: "I've been in England long enough to know that you would want to hear both sides."

He gave Churchill a list of reasons in favor of daylight bombing. The B-17 was designed for it. Our crews were trained for it. We could hit specific targets with precision bombing while the British could continue their attacks on whole industrial cities. But it was a reason near the end of Eaker's list which impressed the Prime Minister most: day *and* night bombing would give the Germans no rest.

When Churchill reported on the Casablanca Conference to the British House of Parliament he stated that the Americans would continue their daylight attacks. Then he glanced up at Ira Eaker sitting in the balcony and said, "We shall bomb those devils around the clock."

By the summer of 1943, after the invasion of Africa had succeeded, large groups of American bombers were again available for attacking the strategic targets far behind the front lines in Europe and the Middle East.

On August 1st, 177 Consolidated B-24 Liberators of the Ninth Air Force took off from bases in Africa on a 2400-mile round-trip flight to bomb the important oil fields at Ploesti, Rumania. Fighter escort was, of course, impossible because of the tremendous distances involved. It was to be a low-level surprise attack, but on the way in some of the planes got lost and the oil fields' strong defenses were alerted. Fifty-four of the B-24s failed to return. Some of those that did, found they had flown so low that cornstalks were stuck in their open bomb bays. For the first time five Congressional Medals of Honor were awarded to men in the same military operation. As

A B-24 Liberator comes in low during the attack on Ploesti.

a result of the attack production of the Ploesti oil fields was cut forty per cent, but the cost had been high—perhaps too high.

In England Ira Eaker was made commander of the Eighth Air Force. With his bomber commander, Fred Anderson, he was making plans to increase their attacks against Germany itself, even though we still had no fighter planes with enough range to protect our bombers all the way.

During the last week in July eighteen targets were

bombed, and while 296 enemy fighters had been shot down, eighty-four B-17s were lost too. Enemy defense was too strong. The number of German Messerschmitt-109 fighters seemed to be increasing.

"We've got to get the Messerschmitt plants," Eaker told Anderson.

It was decided that the destruction of the plant at Regensburg, deep in Germany, was vital. After hitting Regensburg, the B-17s could go on to North Africa, rather than return to England. A second formation of bombers, following directly in the path of the first, was to attack the giant ball-bearing works at Schweinfort. Both missions were to take place on August 17, 1943. "That's the anniversary of our first raid on Rouen," said Anderson.

Colonel Archie Old, the man who later was to set the nonstop, 'round-the-world record in the Air Force's B-52 jet, was to lead the B-17s over Regensburg. At the last moment, however, his division commander, Colonel Curtis LeMay, climbed aboard Old's plane. "Hello, Archie," LeMay said. "You take Number Two plane. I'll go in Number One." He then told the pilot and co-pilot to remain where they were.

He would stand between them, up front, all the way.

Almost from the moment the 126 Flying Fortresses entered Germany they were under severe and prolonged attack by enemy fighter planes. All around him Colonel LeMay could see B-17s being hit and dropping out of formation. All the machine guns on his own Fortress were firing; there was a choking smell of gunpowder in the plane. For three hours the air battle continued. Altogether twenty-four bombers were destroyed. Then, as the formation reached the Messerschmitt plant at Regensburg, the German fighters seemed to disappear. LeMay's Forts made a perfect bomb run over the target. "Bombs away!" Immediately the formation turned south over the Alps and headed for North Africa.

The Germans had expected the Regensburg bombers to return to England, and so most of Colonel LeMay's brave crews escaped further attacks.

The second mission of the day, the formation of 230 B-17s flying towards the ball-bearing factory at Schweinfort, Germany, was hit just as hard as LeMay's had been. The Fortresses could defend themselves better than any other bombers in the skies, but when hundreds of fast fighter planes dived on a Fortress formation some of the B-17s could not escape destruction. This time thirty-six were lost, and many more damaged.

The bomber raids continued, however, although more B-17s were being shot down than could be replaced by the Boeing Company. The climax of this intolerable destruction of our unescorted bombers flying daylight missions occurred on October 14, 1943, when a second raid on Schweinfort was attempted. By this time the Germans had perfected their deadly fighter tactics. While waves of single-engine fighters swept through the bomber formations from the front, twin-engine fighters fired explosive rockets from the rear. Of the 291 bombers sent on the mission, sixty were shot down. The vital ball-bearing works had been hit badly again—but we could not afford to pay the price.

Jimmy Doolittle was brought to England and given command of the Eighth Air Force, and General Carl Spaatz was put in command of a new organization, the United States Strategic Air Forces in Europe. Germany's airpower had to be wiped out. Our bomber losses were too high; moreover, an invasion of the continent would be impossible unless the Allies controlled the air. Hap Arnold wrote to his new commanders: "This is a MUST. . . . Destroy the enemy Air Force wherever you find them . . ."

Despite heavy bombing attacks on German industry, the fighter-plane strength of the *Luftwaffe* was still increasing. Some of these fighter planes could be destroyed by the bristling guns of our Flying Fortresses, but not enough. Only our own fighter aircraft could do the job, but they needed to be able to fly as far as our bombers; the German fighters usually didn't try to intercept a formation of B-17s until its fighter escort had turned back.

By the fall of 1943 American fighter planes such as the P-38 "Lightning" and the big P-47 "Thunderbolt" were flying longer and longer missions with our bombers. This was accomplished by fitting these planes with gas tanks under their bellies. This supply of gas was used first, and the tanks could be dropped off immediately before going into a dogfight.

116

Soon the men in the bombers began calling these protective fighter escorts "Little Friends." Bomber crews learned quickly that if the Little Friends were around they stood a good chance of getting back.

David Schilling, a lieutenant colonel at the age of twenty-five, was one of the many squadron commanders in the Eighth Air Force who became a leading ace while escorting bombers to and from their targets. Dave Schilling belonged to the 56th Fighter Group, often called Zemke's Wolf Pack. By the end of the war its leader, Colonel Hubert Zemke, had himself destroyed twenty-eight enemy planes. But his record was surpassed by several fliers he commanded —pilots like Colonel John C. Meyer, the top ace in the Eighth Air Force, with thirty-seven victories, and Lieutenant Colonel Francis Gabreski, who is credited with thirty-three kills. Then there was Captain Robert S. Johnson, who had more victories in aerial combat than anyone else in Europe except Gabreski.

On the morning of November 26, 1943, Dave Schilling received the squadron orders for the day. The briefing took place at 9:45 A.M. (the bombers the squadron was to protect had already been in the air almost three hours, but the swift fighters would catch up).

Colonel Schilling pointed to a map and told his pilots that they were to furnish support for nine wings of B-17s and B-24s coming home after bombing Bremen, Germany. It was a long trip—the longest the fighters had made to date. The P-47 Thunderbolts would have to fly over 750 miles. All three squadrons of the 56th Group were being used.

At 10:30 Schilling took off. Just as his squadron flew over the Zuider Zee, he spotted contrails up ahead. They belonged to German fighters. Then he saw the Fortresses, and behind and beneath them the burning city of Bremen.

Schilling ordered the belly tanks on the P-47s to be dropped.

While another Zemke squadron attacked the twin-engined German fighters which were shooting rockets into the bombers from the rear, Dave Schilling led his squadron over the Fortresses and Liberators and attacked the single-engine Messerschmitts and Focke-Wulfs which were protecting their slower companions below. In the swirling dogfight which followed, 26 German planes were sent flaming to earth. It was a new record for the pilots of the Eighth Air Force. More important, most of the bombers returned to base safely.

(A little more than a year later, Dave Schilling led his squadron in an attack against 250 German fighters; they shot down thirty-seven enemy planes and Schilling himself destroyed five.)

Zemke's 56th Fighter Group led all other fighter groups in the European Theater in victories until the war was nearly over. Then it was bested by a one-half victory by the remarkable 4th Fighter Group.

Perhaps nothing was more remarkable about the 4th than its leader, Colonel Donald Blakeslee. Don Blakeslee flew more missions (nearly 500) and stayed in continual active combat longer (over 1,000 hours) than any other American fighter pilot. Blakeslee was a superb flier and leader. He could direct his squadrons from the air with the touch of a master. On one mission he was selected to coördinate the operations of the entire Eighth Air Force Fighter Command, which meant that from the air he was controlling almost 800 battle-dispersed planes.

Two of the most famous fighter pilots who served under Blakeslee's command were Captains Don S. Gentile (thirty victories) and John T. Godfrey (thirty-six victories). Gentile and Godfrey flew together, with Godfrey usually acting as wingman, but they both took turns protecting each other. Together they formed a fighter team which Hap Arnold called "the greatest of any war."

Colonel Blakeslee flew on so many combat missions it would be difficult to say which was the most important. Certainly, however, the one he led on March 4, 1944, would be high on almost any list.

A few days before, part of Blakeslee's group had received the first shipment of the new, long-range P-51 fighter, the "Mustang." This remarkable plane could follow the big bombers almost anywhere. The Mustang was what Don Blakeslee had been waiting for.

On the morning of the 4th, he walked into the squadron briefing room where his pilots were already staring excitedly at the long red line drawn across the map deep into Germany.

"Well," Blakeslee said, "you've seen what the show is. Today we're going to Berlin." This was what many fighter pilots had dreamed of; it was also what the Germans said never could happen. "We'll be with the bombers over the target," Blakeslee continued. "And we've been chosen to lead the first formation in over Berlin." Then he told them how the Mustang could get them there and back (over 1,500 miles) even if they had to drop their belly tanks early. There were to be fifty P-51s altogether.

As the Mustangs took off around mid-morning, the bombers were already far ahead (during the beginning and ending of the mission the Fortresses were being escorted by the shorter-ranged Thunderbolts). Many of the Mustangs had to drop out of formation on the way to Berlin; the plane was still so new that not all the "bugs" had been ironed out.

Just after noon, Blakeslee sighted the five wings of B-17s up ahead. He flew on in front of them, weaving back and forth to clear the way for the bombers. Suddenly he saw German fighters below. He rammed his throttle forward and whipped the P-51 over on its back in a screaming dive. The rest of his group followed.

Blakeslee lined up a Messerschmitt in his sights and pressed the gun button on his stick. Nothing happened. His guns were jammed. He pulled up alongside the frightened Messerschmitt pilot and waved at him.

For the rest of the run Don Blakeslee turned his efforts to directing and protecting his own men as they fought to keep the German fighters away from the B-17s. Afterwards he assembled as many P-51s as he could and led them back to England.

The bombing hadn't been the best, it was true, and motor trouble caused half the Mustangs to turn back before they got to the target. But a few American bombers had finally been escorted by American fighters over Berlin. Hermann Goering, the *Reichsmarschall* of the *Luftwaffe,* said later that when he saw the Mustangs over the capital he knew that Germany had as good as lost the war.

Four days later, the team of Don Gentile and John Godfrey were over Berlin themselves. Together they dived into one hundred German planes preparing to attack a formation of B-17s. Between them they de-

(*Left*) Colonel Donald Blakeslee, shortly after escorting the first bombing mission over Berlin.

(*Below*) The greatest fighter pilot team of the war, Captains John T. Godfrey (*left*) and Don S. Gentile, in front of a P-51 Mustang.

stroyed six enemy planes and broke up the attack on the bombers.

As their successes mounted, American fighter pilots began to range far ahead of the bombers, looking for German planes to attack. During February and March more than 800 enemy planes were shot down. The *Luftwaffe* could not stand such losses, and gradually but surely American fliers won control of the air.

Such air superiority was necessary if the planned invasion of the European continent was to be a success. The Air Force was put to work destroying French bridges and railroads leading to the invasion area in Normandy. By D-Day—invasion day, June 6th—76,000 tons of bombs had been dropped on these vital tactical targets.

As Allied troops poured ashore on D-Day and afterwards, scarcely a German plane appeared in the sky to attack the landing forces. In the meantime American bombers had been assigned to destroy the German V-1 sites. The V-1s were small pilotless jet aircraft each carrying a ton of explosive; many had already been sent against England; but now it would be impossible to launch any more.

Waves of bombers also continued their giant 1,000-plane raids against German industry, especially the oil refineries. Despite the heavy bombing of factories, German production increased in some fields; but the lack of oil and gasoline made most of these production gains useless.

After the second invasion of Europe which took place in southern France on August 15th, the Allies began to close in on Germany from all sides. Now, besides bombing and strafing, the Air Force showed its versatility by flying thousands of supply missions and airborne assaults.

On May 7, 1945, Germany surrendered.

The Air Forces had flown a million fighter-plane sorties against Hitler's Europe and more than 75,-000 bomber missions.

In the meantime America was still engaged in a far-flung war on the other side of the world. Here the Air Forces' concept of strategic bombing was to meet its final test.

1942-1945

Hop,
Skip
and Jump

The Boeing B-29 Superfortress had been designed in 1939, two years before the Japanese attack on Pearl Harbor. It often takes many years, however, between the time a modern combat airplane is first put on a drawing board and the time it becomes "operational," meaning ready for combat.

It was not until late March, 1944, that the first giant B-29 was ready for war. By then it was too late to help in Europe; its exceptional long-range capability, however, was exactly what was finally needed in our exhaustive war with Japan.

In the first six months after the war began the Japanese conquerors had swept through the South Pacific. Nothing the relatively small and poorly supplied American, British, Dutch and Australian forces were able to do could stop them. As well as capturing vital strongholds in the Philippines and Malaya and the Netherlands Indies, they had overcome the Mariana Islands and had ranged far south to establish dangerous bases on New Britain, New Guinea and the Solomon Islands which threatened Australia. They also captured Rangoon and then invaded most of Burma, cutting off China from her allies in India.

Japan now had much of the empire she had dreamed of conquering, but it was difficult to hold. Allied aircraft and submarines immediately set about destroying the shipping Japan needed to supply and protect her new "colonies."

In early May, 1942, immediately after Jimmy Doolittle's surprise raid on Tokyo from the aircraft carrier *Hornet,* the Japanese met with their first real defeat in a naval engagement called the Battle of the Coral Sea. A more important battle occurred a month later near Midway Island. A powerful Japanese fleet including six battleships and four aircraft carriers was defeated when all the enemy carriers were sunk by Navy planes based on three American carriers. It was a naval battle which took place mostly in the air. The Japanese battleships were helpless without air protection. Airpower would rule the seas thereafter.

In the meantime the Allied forces in Australia, under the command of General Douglas MacArthur, had been slowly rebuilding their strength to strike back. The plan was to recapture the various islands which led north like giant stepping stones to Japan itself, which was too far away to be directly attacked. Sometimes each island, as the Allies came to it, would be taken. Sometimes one island—or several islands —would be skipped over, leaving the Japanese forces on it cut off and surrounded while our Marines,

Army, Navy and Army Air Forces attacked another vital point farther north.

None of this would be possible, however, unless Air Force, Navy and Marine pilots won control of the air. Then we would not only be free to make landings in force on these islands, but we would also be able to prevent the Japanese from reinforcing their own troops already there.

First our bombers (B-17s and smaller two-engined Mitchell B-25s and Martin B-26s specially fitted with extra machine guns packed into their noses) attacked Japanese airfields on New Guinea and helped stall the intended invasion of Australia. Then, on August 7th, the Marines made their first important island landing against the enemy. The island chosen was Guadalcanal in the Solomons. On it was Henderson Field, an air base necessary for further advance. When American ships and planes destroyed eleven Japanese transports bringing desperately needed reinforcements in November, victory on Guadalcanal was certain.

By this time, too, Air Force pilots had received a new fighter plane destined to make history in the

South Pacific. This was the twin-tailed Lockheed P-38 "Lightning."

The Lightning was faster than any Japanese plane; its twin engines also gave it greater power and reliability. It was not as maneuverable as the Japanese Zero fighter—no American plane was—but in the right hands it outfought everything the enemy had.

Major Richard I. Bong, our all-time ace, flew a Lightning. Dick Bong had not been fighting in the South Pacific long before he was made flight leader of the Flying Knights Squadron. The Flying Knights destroyed ten Japanese planes for every P-38 they lost. By the time Dick Bong had flown 146 missions with the Knights he had shot down twenty-eight Japanese planes, surpassing Eddie Rickenbacker's record by two.

Bong was then sent back to the United States to help train cadets at gunnery school. He wanted to get back to the war, however, and he finally persuaded his superiors to send him to the Pacific as an advanced gunnery instructor. Even though he was supposed to be a "noncombatant" he managed to flame twelve more enemy aircraft, bringing his total

Major Richard I. Bong, ace of aces, in the cockpit of his P-38 Lightning. The Japanese flags painted on his plane indicate that at the time of this picture Bong had shot down a total of 27 enemy planes.

to forty victories. When he was asked why he kept getting into combat when he was supposed to be instructing, Dick Bong only said, ". . . demonstration is a pretty good way of teaching."

The second leading ace in the Far East Theater was Major Thomas B. McGuire. Like Bong, he too flew a P-38. Tommy McGuire went to the South

Pacific near the beginning of 1943. Once he shot down four Zeros in one day; another time three. By Christmas of 1944 he had thirty-eight victories. A few days later his plane accidentally stalled during a dogfight and McGuire was killed in the crash.

Both Richard Bong and Thomas McGuire were awarded the Congressional Medal of Honor.

Besides being the fighter plane responsible for destroying more Japanese aircraft than any other, the P-38 Lightning took part in the most daring interceptor raid of the war.

On April 17, 1943, U. S. Navy radio monitors picked up a coded message which outlined an air inspection tour Admiral Yamamoto was to make of Japanese bases the following day. Yamamoto was the military genius responsible for most of Japan's early victories. He planned the attack at Pearl Harbor. Under his leadership the Japanese fleets had defeated superior American fleets four times during the bitter struggle for Guadalcanal. Admiral Yamamoto was possibly the most dangerous man in the Pacific.

The Secretary of the Navy, Frank Knox, thought it might be possible to intercept Yamamoto on his routine inspection tour and shoot him down. Knox called in Hap Arnold who in turn discussed the problem with Charles Lindbergh, now an authority on the P-38. It was decided that if the P-38s could be fitted immediately with special auxiliary gas tanks they might be able to fly from Guadalcanal and intercept Yamamoto over Kahili airfield, 550 miles away. This meant a round trip of more than one thousand miles for the Lightnings. Moreover, the Admiral's plane would be heavily guarded by many Zeros.

Late on the afternoon of April 17th Major John Mitchell, commander of the 339th Squadron, was told of the plan, and later that evening four B-24 Liberators from Port Moresby flew in with thirty-six auxiliary tanks. Mechanics worked all night fitting them to Mitchell's planes.

Early the next morning, sixteen P-38s were on their way from Guadalcanal to intercept Yamamoto. Captain Thomas Lamphier, Jr., was to lead four P-38s in direct attack on Yamamoto's plane while Major Mitchell and the rest of the squadron covered them from above.

Several hours later, as the P-38s neared Kahili, Lamphier sighted two Japanese bombers with a fighter escort. In one of those bombers rode Admiral Yamamoto. Lamphier chose the bomber most heavily guarded and began his attack. Only his wingman, Rex Barber, followed him in. (One of the other P-38 pilots couldn't eject his belly tank, and he and his wingman had to turn away from the fight.)

While Barber took on most of the escort, Tom Lamphier dived through the formation. He shot down one Zero and then caught up with Yamamoto. More Zeros were after him now but Lamphier kept on. He got the bomber in his sights and pressed the trigger. Bullets ripped across the bomber's right wing, setting it on fire. It crashed into the jungle, killing all of its occupants. Tom Lamphier barely got away alive.

Once Guadalcanal was firmly in American hands, Marine and Army troops began to move northward to retake the rest of the islands in the Solomons. From the air the Thirteenth Air Force swept on ahead, destroying Japanese planes and airfields wherever they could find them.

In the early part of the war particularly, the Japanese soldier, sailor or pilot was a formidable, well-trained foe. Only the bravest and strongest could best him. On the land, the sea, and in the air, Americans showed they possessed these qualities.

On June 16, 1943, for instance, a lone B-17 was sent to the northern Solomons to try to photograph new Japanese airfields. Its pilot was Captain Jay Zeamer, Jr. The mission proceeded according to plan over one Japanese base after another until the B-17 approached Buka, one of the strongest enemy airfields.

Up ahead twenty Zero fighters took off from Buka to attack the Fortress. Zeamer knew the B-17 could not fight off that many planes, but he also knew photographs of Buka were desperately needed. The Fort flew on, taking pictures. Then it was too late to turn back.

The Zeros pressed simultaneous attacks from the front and sides. Machine-gun bullets and exploding cannon shells raked the lone B-17. Zeamer was hit, and so were three gunners and the bombardier, Joseph Sarnoski, who was manning a nose gun.

The Fortress itself was riddled. Control wires were cut, oxygen tanks punctured, and hydraulic lines split open. When the Zeros began their second onslaught a cannon shell exploded in Sarnoski's nose compartment, wounding him fatally, but he stayed at his gun and broke up the frontal attack.

Although six Zeros had been downed by the guns of the Fortress, the Japanese pilots would not give up. Zeamer, badly wounded, continued to maneuver the crippled giant to give his gunners the best shots. Once he even dived the huge four-engine bomber after a banking Zero, firing the single nose gun from his pilot's seat until the enemy fighter caught fire.

Finally when ten Zeros had been shot down, the others called off the attack. Jay Zeamer could no longer fly the B-17 himself. A nineteen-year-old gunner took over the controls because the co-pilot was unconscious; Zeamer directed the gunner as he flew the Fortress back to the base.

Doctors were amazed that Captain Zeamer was

still alive; they picked more than 120 pieces of steel out of his body. Both he and bombardier Sarnoski were awarded the Medal of Honor.

By the beginning of 1944 the Japanese hold on the Solomon Islands was broken and attacks against enemy strong points on New Guinea were stepped up. With strong Fifth Air Force support, the small islands north of New Guinea and the Solomons were captured, cutting off all hope of rescue for the 80,000 Japanese troops isolated in the jungles. Now plans were made for the liberation of the Philippines.

In the meantime the first B-29 Superfortresses were arriving in the Far East. These big brothers of the famous B-17 had a remarkable combat radius of 1,600 miles. Unfortunately we had no bases of our own that close to Japan early in 1944.

China still had fields close enough to Japan for the B-29s, but the problems of supplying bases there were immense. The B-29s had to fly their own fuel, explosives and supplies over The Hump. On May 27 the B-29s made their first raid against Bang-

kok. Soon they were bombing Japan itself. In August
Curtis LeMay, now a major general, arrived in
China to take command of the B-29s. He insisted
on breaking the rule that no commanding officer be
allowed to fly on the missions. "I've got to go along,"
he told Hap Arnold, "or I'll never know what I'm
up against." LeMay immediately began toughening
up the "training" program.

The B-29 crews knew that these missions from
China were only the first steps in the overall plan.
The Superfortresses really needed bases in the Mariana Islands, which lay only 1,500 miles southeast of
the Japanese mainland. But these islands, now in the
enemy's possession, had to be invaded and captured
first, as did the Gilbert and Marshall islands which
led up to the Marianas.

Strong detachments of Marines and Army troops
landed on the islands, backed by overwhelming
forces of the United States Navy, especially carrier
planes. By the summer of 1944 the main islands in
the Marianas—Saipan, Tinian, Guam—were taken.
(In one battle off the Marianas, Navy fliers shot
down more than 300 Japanese carrier-based planes

in a single day, with only small losses to themselves.) Almost immediately bulldozers began to carve five gigantic landing strips for the Superfortresses.

On November 24, the first formation of 111 B-29s took off from Saipan and headed for Tokyo. At their head was Brigadier General Rosy O'Donnell, who, three years before, had tried to do what he could to save the Philippines. The weather was bad and the bombing poor, but this was the first raid on Tokyo since Jimmy Doolittle's.

Then, two months later, Curtis LeMay was brought to the Marianas from China to see that "maximum effort" was applied to the operation.

It was still a long way from Saipan to Tokyo. A damaged B-29 often couldn't make it back—and there was no place to land except the ocean. There was a Japanese-held island, however, halfway between Japan and the B-29 bases. It was called Iwo Jima.

Air Force B-24s bombed the island for almost three weeks before the Marines landed on February 19, 1945. The Japanese resistance was fanatical. It took the Marines four weeks to capture Iwo Jima in one

Major General Curtis LeMay made one of the major decisions of the war when he sent B-29 bombers (*below*) over Japan at low altitudes.

of the bloodiest battles in the Pacific. Almost 5,000 Marines lost their lives. But during the rest of the war, about 2,400 B-29s carrying 25,000 crewmen made emergency landings on Iwo Jima.

By 1945 Air Force planners had become convinced that fire bomb raids against Japan, rather than high explosives, would cause the most damage to her tinderbox cities. A few such raids had been tried but the results had been poor because of high winds or bad weather. Then Curtis LeMay made one of the major decisions of the war. He decided to send his bombers over Japan at low altitudes. They were to navigate singly, not in formation. Coming in low, their accuracy would increase, they would need less gas, and they could carry more incendiaries.

This plan was a complete reversal of everything the Air Force had believed in. But, LeMay said, this was a different problem. Japan's industry, for instance, was spread out over whole cities. Enemy fighter strength wasn't as strong in Japan as it was over Europe, either.

The first attack took place on March 9th, when 334 B-29s came in low over Tokyo. The incendiary bombs started such a holocaust that the heat from the roaring flames flipped two B-29s over on their backs. One pilot said that "Tokyo caught fire like a forest of pine trees." Almost sixteen square miles were burned out in the heart of the city.

More Japanese cities were hit in the same way—Nagoya, Osaka, Kobe. . . . As the raids became more and more successful, B-29 losses dropped.

Almost seventy more cities were burned. The destruction was unbelievable. On a second fire raid over Tokyo the updraft threw a piece of metal roofing 16,000 feet in the air and struck the wing of a Superfortress.

Horrible as these fire raids were, pilots knew that unless Japan were brought to her knees by attacks from the air so that an invasion of the home islands would not be necessary, hundreds of thousands of Americans would lose their lives.

Less than three hundred miles to the south of Japan, American forces were preparing for the invasion which General Arnold still hoped would not be necessary. The capture of Okinawa provided sites for new bases, and General Ennis Whitehead's Fifth

Air Force advanced northward from the retaken Philippines. General Thomas D. White's Seventh Air Force moved to Okinawa.

Then, in late summer, came an explosion which astounded the world. There were several Japanese cities which had remained relatively untouched by the fire bombs. One of these was Hiroshima. Early on the morning of August 6th, 1945, Colonel Paul Tibbets, Jr., took off from Tinian in his B-29, *Enola Gay*. At 9:15 the bomb bays opened and a giant cylindrical object dropped toward Hiroshima. The crew of the *Enola Gay* put on green goggles. Fifty seconds later a fantastic, unbelievable blast erupted below, covering the whole city. Then a gigantic cloud mushroomed up 50,000 feet above the destruction.

Seventy thousand persons were dead. But Japan still did not surrender.

Another atomic bomb was dropped, this time on Nagasaki.

Japan surrendered on August 10th.

After seven long years of conflict the world was once more at peace.

1948

Highway in the Sky: The Berlin Airlift

After Germany was defeated, it was occupied by the Allies. Russia controlled eastern Germany while the United States, England and France governed the western part. Unfortunately Germany's capital city, Berlin, was in the Russian Zone. Because of its importance, however, Berlin was also divided up, with the Americans, British and French taking over West Berlin.

This meant, of course, that West Berlin was completely surrounded by Russian forces. And these seemed to be growing more and more unfriendly.

In 1948 the Russians decided to take steps to try to force the Western Allies out of Berlin. Under various pretexts, they closed all highway traffic to the city. They stopped trains by saying that the tracks needed repairs. The only way left to reach West Berlin was by airplane. (The Russians had guaranteed the free use of three twenty-mile-wide air corridors which led from Berlin to the American and British Zones.)

It looked as if the Western Allies would have to get out. If they stayed, they would be responsible for supplying a city of more than 2,000,000 people with everything it needed for survival by the one means left, the airplane.

Such a gigantic task had never been attempted before by air. Many people thought it would be impossible. It would take at least 4,500 *tons* of food, fuel and medicine *a day* to keep Berlin alive.

145

Immediately after the Russian blockade went into effect, however, General Lucius B. Clay, the American military governor in Berlin, called in General Curtis LeMay, who was now in command of the U. S. Air Force in Europe.

Clay told Curtis LeMay that the Western Allies were not going to leave. Berlin would be supplied by air, and LeMay would have to begin setting up an airlift at once. There was only a limited reserve of food left.

On Sunday, June 26, LeMay loaded every available transport and headed it towards the blockaded city. Many of the pilots who flew to Berlin that day had had desk jobs the day before. But by that evening eighty tons of medicine, milk and food had been flown into Tempelhof Air Base near the city. It was nowhere nearly enough, but it was a beginning.

On that same Sunday LeMay also sent out a request for more planes and crews. They came from all over the world—from the Philippines, Guam, Texas and Alaska. The British also provided planes. In the next few days Wiesbaden Air Base near Frankfort became crowded with the new arrivals.

LeMay put them right to work, under the command of General William H. Tunner, who would run the airlift.

And work was the word for it. Flying the Berlin Airlift—dubbed "Operation Vittles" by the Americans—was a round-the-clock job. Army trucks carried the vital supplies to the waiting planes, which were always overloaded because of the crisis. Aviation gas for the flight was delivered to Germany in huge quantities by Navy tankers. As soon as each plane was loaded it took off for Berlin.

The planes flew only three minutes apart. The weather was often bad, especially as winter came on. Thousands of times pilots had to bring in their dangerously heavy planes "blind." On the ground, skilled radar operators picked out the planes coming in through the thick fog, rain or snow. As each ship neared Tempelhof, the operator guided the pilot to the field, closer and closer, until the runway was right under him and he could let down safely. If the plane missed the field or came in too high or perhaps too far to one side, it had to turn around and head all the way back to its take-off point. The air was too crowded with other transports to risk another try.

Once the plane was on the ground, the pilot and his crew grabbed a cup of coffee and perhaps a sandwich while the cargo was loaded into waiting trucks. Then the plane took off again immediately. Most of the crews made two trips a day.

By 1949 Operation Vittles was in full swing. More than 300 C-54 transports, as well as many other types of aircraft, were being used by the Air Force. The R. A. F. was working night and day, too. The daily tonnage requirement was being met—and even bettered. Several new airports had been built to accommodate the hundreds of flights a day.

But there was danger too. Thirty-one Americans lost their lives in twelve crashes. Still, this figure was low, considering the number of planes and flights involved. And the whole operation was so skillfully carried out that there was only one mid-air collision.

The West Berliners, our enemies only a few years before, applauded what the Americans and British were doing. They gathered by the hundreds every day at the three unloading fields and cheered the planes as they landed. Lieutenant Gail S. Halvorsen noticed that there were often many children in these groups. Unofficially he started a new operation called "Little Vittles." As he came in for a landing he and his crew dropped candy and chewing gum attached to tiny parachutes to the waiting children. Operation Little Vittles was taken up by scores of other pilots.

The Russians, who had made fun of the Berlin Airlift at first, finally began to see that the blockade was never going to drive the Western Allies out of Berlin. Not only had airpower won the first big battle in the new "cold war," but as a result of it the free Germans in Berlin found something they thought they had lost forever: the courage to face the future.

1950-1953

Battle of the Jets: Korea

Eight miles above the barren mountains of Korea, several flights of sleek North American F-86 "Sabrejets" weave slowly back and forth in the thin atmosphere. They are hunters, looking for enemy jet fighters, the Russian-built MIG-15.

Many of the Air Force pilots flying these new F-86

Sabrejets are veteran aces of World War II. Experienced hands and cool heads are needed in jet combat. The temperature at 40,000 feet is about sixty below zero. The pilot must breathe pure oxygen under pressure, or he would die in a few minutes. The sky above him is dark blue, making it difficult to see an enemy plane. The pilot keeps turning his head from one side to the other, on the lookout.

The F-86—like any jet fighter—is a complex mechanism. The pilot has 100 controls to operate and twenty-four instruments to watch, plus a dozen lights to warn him of trouble somewhere. Around him run cables, hydraulic lines, wires, fuel lines, cooling and heating ducts, oxygen tubes. Just behind him is a giant, roaring blowtorch, the jet itself, with as much power as three locomotives. And he is streaking through the air at nearly six hundred miles an hour.

The "hunters" have already flown more than 200 miles from their base in South Korea and now they are nearing the border between North Korea and Manchuria which is marked by the Yalu River. On the other side of this river the Chinese Communists

A group of F-86 Sabrejets streak toward enemy territory in northwest Korea.

have built their air bases. Our pilots cannot cross this river to attack the Chinese because we do not want to carry the war beyond the borders of Korea. So the F-86s wait south of the Yalu in an area called "MIG Alley" for the Chinese pilots to bring their Russian MIGs to battle.

Suddenly the F-86 pilots see swarms of dust trails

lifting from the enemy airfields across the Yalu. The MIGs have taken up the challenge. They are coming up to meet the Sabrejets.

Over the radio, the pilots hear reports from other flights along the Yalu:

"Twenty-four taking off at Antung," calls the leader.

"I make it fifty over here at Takushan," yells another.

"I see only twelve up north," says a third.

"Don't worry. There'll be enough for everybody."

The Sabrejets wait for the MIGs to gain altitude and cross the river (already more MIGs are taking off from the protected fields below).

"Here they come!" the flight leader radios.

The F-86s turn head-on into the swarm of MIGs. Scores of auxiliary wing tanks fall through the air like silver minnows, as the Sabres drop them to gain extra speed and maneuverability. The jets roar straight at one another, guns blazing; their closing speed is an incredible 1,200 miles an hour. The Sabrejets cut through the enemy formation and a MIG flies into pieces. None of the F-86s are hit.

Now individual planes of both sides break to the right and left. The battle has become a free-for-all. The MIG-15 is an excellent plane. It is fast and can actually climb higher than our jets. But our pilots are better. Our gunnery is better too.

A favorite trick of the Sabre pilots is to let the Chinese flier think he's closing in for the kill from behind. Suddenly the F-86 turns sharply to the left and the right, and then slams on his air brakes. The MIG cannot follow the tight maneuver and flies past his target. Then the Sabrejet pilot closes his air brakes and pounces on the tail of the surprised MIG, all guns firing.

From the ground the battle of the jets looks like long strings of white yarn, snarled here and there, strung across the sky. The hot exhaust from the jets leaves white contrails in the cold atmosphere.

In a few minutes the MIGs have had enough. They turn for the Yalu. The Sabrejets, now low on fuel, head home too. One F-86 pilot radios that his plane has been hit and that his engine may quit. It does, but he's high enough so that he can glide to the Yellow Sea and bail out safely.

The score for this typical day: ten MIGs shot down; only one Sabrejet missing.

How did the conflict in Korea start?

This little country jutting out from the coast of Manchuria had long been under the heel of Japan. After World War II, Korea (like Germany) was divided up, supposedly for a short time; in this case the new temporary military governments were just Russia and the United States. Both promised to let the United Nations hold free elections in a reasonable length of time.

North Korea, however, which was soon controlled by both Russia and Red China, was never permitted free elections. Instead, under Communist direction, it prepared for war against its southern neighbors.

On June 25, 1950, the North Koreans attacked the Republic of Korea.

At first the North Koreans overwhelmed the small garrisons of Republic of Korea and American troops in their way; but our Fifth Air Force, flying P-51s and other World War II aircraft, proved to be more than a match for the Communist pilots. Soon we almost controlled the air over Korea.

Air Force B-29s, under the command of Major General Emmett O'Donnell, carried out strategic attacks against many industrial targets in North Korea. At times the bombers even helped our fighter planes break up strong infantry attacks against the outnumbered United Nations troops on the ground, which were being driven farther and farther south. On September 3rd, for example, General Kean, commander of the 25th Division, said that "the close air support strikes rendered by the Fifth Air Force again saved Division, as they have many times before."

In spite of the fact that the North Koreans had forced us to retreat at first, they were not able to remain on the offensive. Our fighters and bombers had cut off their supplies and wrecked their production.

On September 15, United States troops under the command of General MacArthur made a surprise invasion at Inchon, halfway up the Korean coast. The demoralized North Korean army fled, and within a month we had retaken all lost ground.

Now the United Nations troops continued their advance toward the Yalu River, capturing Pyongyang, capital of the North Korean Government. By November, however, there was strong indication that the Chinese Communists weren't going to let United Nations troops get to the Yalu. The first MIG-15 jet fighters were crossing the river and attacking UN planes. On November 8 the first all-jet air battle in history took place. The MIGs tangled with Air Force F-80 jets, and in spite of the fact that the old F-80s were outclassed by the modern MIG-15s, Lieutenant Russel Brown shot down one—the first Communist jet plane destroyed in the Korean War.

Suddenly Chinese ground troops crossed the Yalu River by the hundreds of thousands. Once again United Nations forces were forced to retreat. And once again the Fifth Air Force had the vital job of protecting the troops as they fell back.

This time, however, the UN troops were stronger and better supplied. They withdrew only halfway down the Korean peninsula and then dug in. New F-86 Sabrejets were brought in to match the swift MIGs.

The Chinese threw wave after wave of troops at the United Nations defenders, but against concentrated fire from the ground and the air these attacks failed. Then the UN forces began moving north again toward the 38th parallel, the original dividing line between North and South Korea.

The Communists knew they were beaten and asked for immediate cease-fire discussions. But as the talks went on, the Chinese used the time to rebuild their weakened forces. It was obvious that as soon as they were strong again they would attack once more.

The Fifth Air Force as well as planes of the Navy were given the task of destroying the major railway connection in North Korea. The Chinese Communists in turn knew that if they were to continue their build-up they would have to destroy us in the air. They sent over a thousand MIG-15 fighters against a much smaller number of F-86 Sabres. And so began a great aerial battle.

America's first all-jet ace was Captain James Jabara, who had already shot down four German planes in World War II. He destroyed his fourth and fifth MIGs on the same day, May 20, 1951. By the end of the war Captain Jabara was our second ranking fighter pilot in Korea with fifteen MIGs to his credit.

Strangely enough our top jet ace almost never got to Korea. He was Captain Joseph McConnell, Jr. Captain McConnell had been in World War II, also —as a navigator in a B-24. He had always wanted to be a fighter pilot, however, and after the war he reapplied for training in our first jet, the Lockheed F-80 "Shooting Star." He was in Alaska when the Korean War began, and he tried again and again to be transferred to battle. Finally, in the fall of 1952, his request was granted.

Within a month after Captain McConnell had shot down his first MIG, he became an ace. Once his Sabrejet was struck by anti-aircraft fire and he had to bail out. He landed in enemy waters but was rescued immediately by a UN helicopter. The next day he destroyed his eighth MIG.

Then, on the morning of May 18, Joe McConnell flamed two MIG fighters. That afternoon he went up again and bagged a third. His score was now sixteen deadly MIG-15s destroyed in air-to-air combat. It was the highest score of the war.

Of the 839 MIGs shot down over Korea, 792 of them fell under the blazing guns of American F-86 Sabrejets. Only seventy-eight Sabrejets were lost. It was a remarkable ten-to-one record from any point of view, and it proved to the world again the excellence of the fliers in the U. S. Air Force.

And while the MIGs were being blasted from the skies, American bombers continued to hit vital targets in North Korea. The truce negotiations were getting nowhere, and more pressure had to be applied to bring the talks to a close.

United Nations aircraft hit North Korea's giant hydroelectric plants, knocking out ninety per cent of her electric power. Then Republic F-84 jet fighters hit the Toksan and Chasan irrigation dams, flooding important road and rail communications.

The Communists were ready for an armistice. The hostilities were over. Korea was still divided, but the United Nations had stopped armed aggression. And airpower had again played a crucial role in world affairs.

Modern Minutemen— SAC, TAC, and ADC

Surprise attacks have always been a part of war, and they always will be. But until the mid-twentieth century such attacks were of limited, short-lived value. The country attacked suffered an initial setback, but very often it had ample time to recover.

The Japanese sneak bombing of Pearl Harbor, for

instance, destroyed a great deal of America's military might; but we had time not only to replace what we had lost but also to build an Army, Navy and Air Force which were the largest and most powerful in our history.

Today the situation is different. Today one jet bomber can carry more destructive power than was carried by all Allied bombers in World War II. And the jet bomber can fly anywhere in the world.

What does this mean? It means that America must be able at all times to defend itself in a matter of minutes. It also means that we must be ready to launch a counterattack the moment we are certain we are being attacked.

As you are reading this, the three combat arms of the Air Force—the Air Defense Command (ADC), the Strategic Air Command (SAC), and the Tactical Air Command (TAC)—are ready for war. They have to be. If an "unidentified flying object" is discovered by the powerful radar net which surrounds the United States and Canada, it must be intercepted. If it is an enemy it must be destroyed before it reaches us. There will be no time to make plans or load and arm planes, much less call up reserves or train new men.

The Air Force believes that an all-out nuclear war would last no more than two or three days.

Across the top of the American continent just inside the Arctic Circle runs a 9,000-mile chain of radar stations called the DEW (Distant Early Warning) Line; by sea and air it extends from the Azores to Hawaii. Below it is another band of radar stations called the Mid-Canada Line; farther south, along the northern border of the United States, is still another radar screen called the Pine Tree Line.

Off the east and west coasts of North America there are floating radar posts called Texas Towers; these areas are patrolled by Air Force and Navy planes as well as by ships carrying radar. (Important cities in America are further protected by the Army's Nike-Hercules nuclear surface-to-air missile.)

This giant, intricate network of radar warning stations is under a joint U.S.-Canadian command called North American Air Defense (NORAD), of which the Air Defense Command of the Air Force is a major part.

Suppose an unidentified "blip" is picked up on the screen of one of these radar outposts. If no friendly aircraft are known to be in the area, local ADC bases are alerted. Pilots run to their jet interceptors which are waiting, already armed and fueled. The North American Air Defense Command has eighty squadrons of all-weather fighter-interceptors, including the Convair F-102A "Delta Dagger" and the world's fastest fighter, the Lockheed F-104A "Starfighter." Many of these planes are armed with the uncanny Falcon missiles which can "see" their target and guide themselves to it.

In minutes the planes are in the air, climbing toward the radar contact. As the jets approach within range of the powerful radar station which is tracking the unidentified blip, the ground station directs the interceptors toward their target by radio. As soon as the jets are close enough, they pick up the blip on their own radar sets. If the interceptor jets discover that the "unknown" plane is a friendly one, they radio this information back to base; if not the interceptor pilot turns on his automatic radar tracking device which is connected to the Falcon missiles his supersonic jet carries.

At the proper moment, the missiles fire automatically and direct themselves to the target either by radar or the heat rays given off by the enemy jet. They are unerring. It is possible that the interceptor pilot might never see the plane he has destroyed.

At the same time the unidentified blip was originally discovered by our radar net, this information was immediately relayed to General Laurence S. Kuter's North American Air Defense Command headquarters at Colorado Springs, Colorado. Within seconds, "hot-line" telephones have sent this information to the headquarters of the Strategic Air Command in Nebraska, and to the Joint Chiefs of Staff in Washington.

The nerve-center of SAC is an underground three-story "blockhouse" not far from Omaha; it is a combination command post, weather station and com-

mand center. It is bomb-proof; the chart room is
hundreds of feet long. The radar reports from
NORAD are watched carefully here. If the "unknown" begins to get too close, SAC sends a special
alert to all its bases. No chances are taken. Bombers
must not be caught on the ground; they must be on
their way even before the enemy strikes us.

There is a red telephone at SAC headquarters. In
seconds it connects to more than forty SAC Command
bases in the United States. Within minutes every
available medium B-47 and heavy B-52 bomber can
be in the air, aimed at a predetermined target. The
hundreds of bombers already in the air on training
missions all over the world are contacted by special
single-sideband radio.

If General Thomas S. Power, the Commander in
Chief, decides the "unknown" is getting too close,
he orders Alert Red. At this moment SAC is at war.
SAC crews all over the globe run to their ships.
They have been waiting in full combat uniform;
the only things they are allowed to take off are their
shoes. The first bombers are off the ground in three

At SAC headquarters officers and airmen post fresh information on the map panels in the operations control room, while
(*below*) alert pilots rush to their aircraft in response to a
warning buzzer.

minutes. These planes will automatically turn back to base after a time—unless they receive confirmation that America really is being attacked.

The Strategic Air Command has been called "the great deterrent." For more than a decade its mighty fleet of jet bombers, all armed with nuclear weapons and capable of flying nonstop to any place in the world, have helped keep the peace. If we have the planes and the men to inflict terrible damage on the enemy, the chances are he will never attack, no matter how much he can hurt us. SAC says that once it is forced to drop a bomb in retaliation it will have failed in its mission.

SAC was formed after World War II. Its first commander was General George Kenney, who set up the organization for the task ahead. In 1948 General Curtis LeMay took over, and in less than ten years he built SAC into the greatest organization of its kind the world has ever seen. He also pioneered the startling idea of putting our armed forces on a war-time footing even though we were at peace. Today the important SAC team is headed by General

Power, whose leadership has enabled it to meet the challenges of the coming Space Age.

In spite of the size of the organization and the scope of its operations (SAC commands more multi-engined planes than all the major airlines in the free world) comparatively few civilians have ever seen a jet bomber. To most people SAC is just a word. The Russians know about it, however. They too have a strategic air force.

The third member of the Air Force's combat team is the Tactical Air Command.

TAC is the most versatile of all the commands. Part of its job is to complement SAC in air offensive and aid ADC during the defensive phase of all-out war. But it is also equipped and trained to destroy tactical targets—railways, bridges, gun emplacements and enemy troops.

The Tactical Air Command was the force which carried much of the fight in Korea, for instance.

The command, now under General O. P. Weyland, has as its basic fighter plane the first of the "century series," the supersonic North American F-100 "Supersabre." It also has a wing of McDonald F-101 "Voodoos."

The new Republic F-105 "Thunderchief" fighter-bomber is now being added to TAC. Designed especially for tactical work, the F-105 has an internal bomb rack and an aerial refueling system. It is also equipped with the deadly Sidewinder air-to-air missile and the Vulcan, the world's fastest firing cannon. With the F-105, TAC will have a global capability. A tactical version of the speed king, the F-104, is also being produced for General Weyland's command.

One of the most spectacular maneuvers used by TAC pilots comes in executing its Low-Altitude Bombing System, more familiarly known as "toss bombing." A fighter pilot cannot drop an atom bomb from a high altitude with accuracy. Yet if he drops it from a low altitude he's likely to be caught in the bomb blast.

TAC has solved the problem by having the pilot come in low toward the target. Once he is over it, he points his fighter straight up. Then the bomb is automatically released while the plane is in a vertical position. Momentum carries the bomb straight on up in the air while the pilot flips his ship over on its back and then executes an Immelmann roll, diving away from the target area. By the time the A-bomb comes down the pilot is miles away.

The mission of the Tactical Air Command grows more complex every year. Thanks to the pioneering work in air-to-air refueling of pilots like the late SAC Colonel Dave Schilling, TAC fighter aircraft now have a long-range ability to fly across the oceans. Using booster rockets they can, on the other hand, take off from launcher racks on the backs of trucks.

From troop-carrying and close air support to air-to-air combat and nuclear bombing TAC can do the job. In combination with SAC and ADC, it helps make up a "force-in-being" to defend the free world.

Today these vital commands, as well as their many companion support commands, are combat-ready because the Air Force believes in planning well into the future.

Much of the future potential of the Air Force will depend on how well the Air Research and Development Command (ARDC) does its job. ARDC's mission is to provide the basic research for the weapons of tomorrow. At Cape Canaveral, Florida, for instance, the missilemen of ARDC carry out 'round-the-clock tests on new "birds." Every experimental plane, every gun, every rocket the Air Force might want to use either now or many years from now is this command's responsibility.

The test pilots who fly for ARDC are the Magellans of the modern world. Fliers like Captain Charles Yeager, who first broke the "sound barrier" in the rocket-propelled Bell X-1, and Ivan Kincheloe, who took the X-2 to a record-breaking height of 126,000 feet, are men who have already helped to broaden the ever-widening horizons of speed and space.

The life of a test pilot is a dangerous one calling for exceptional courage as well as extraordinary mental and physical ability. Take as an example the career of Lieutenant Colonel Frank Everest. An ace in World War II, Colonel Everest was later assigned to the Flight Test Center at Edwards Air Force Base, California.

Everest had many close calls with death, but he always stayed with his test ship as long as possible and brought back valuable information. More than once experimental airplanes have blown up as he was flying them; twice the rockets of the X-1 exploded while he was at the controls. Once the pressurized canopy on the X-1 cracked at 63,000 feet and Colonel Everest was saved only by the T-1 pressure suit he was wearing.

What Colonel Everest and his fellow test pilots discover about the new frontiers of space is vitally important to the Air Force. But ARDC is also concerned with more immediate problems.

Already, for instance, giant ballistic-missile early-warning radar stations—with antennas as big as football fields—are under construction for NORAD in Greenland and the Aleutian Islands. These powerful detectors have a range of more than 3,500 miles.

The Air Defense Command is also installing a new guidance system for its interceptors. Through a complex electronics system hook-up to all the radar stations in a given area, the interceptor is automatically guided to its target and its missiles fired.

All the pilot has to do is take off and land.

SAC is now arming its new bomber, the B-52G, with two North American "Hound Dog" missiles under its wings which can be released hundreds of miles from the target. The Strategic Air Command has also been put in charge of the 1st Missile Division, which will include the Atlas and Titan Intercontinental Ballistic Missiles, and the Jupiter and Thor Intermediate Range Ballistic Missiles.

Missiles cannot replace the manned bomber for a long time, but they can supplement it. As yet only a bomber can find its target with certainty, or attack a different target if necessary. Only a bomber can assess the damage it has done. And only a bomber can be called back in time if the "unknown" blip turns out to be friendly.

SAC is at present in transition from a bomber to a mixed bomber-missile force. Undoubtedly the immediate future will bring many radical changes in the Air Force. Perhaps someday SAC will be renamed the Strategic Space Command. If so, it will be ready.

West Point of the Air

Almost from the very beginning of the Air Age it was the dream of men like Billy Mitchell that America should have an independent air arm. For thirty years, however, their dream remained no more than that. The Air Force had changed and grown in importance tremendously since the days of the

Wright brothers. It had been called by many names
—the Aeronautical Division, Aviation Section, Air
Service, Air Corps, and Army Air Forces. But it was
not until September, 1947, that the United States
Air Force was established on a coequal basis with
the Army and Navy.

As in the past, however, many of the officers in
the new Air Force still had to be graduates of either
West Point or Annapolis. Obviously such a system
was not satisfactory to anyone.

On April 1, 1954, the establishment of the Air
Force Academy was authorized. Three months later
the Secretary of the Air Force chose 18,000 acres of
ranchland just west of the Rocky Mountains near
Colorado Springs, Colorado, as the site of the Academy. While the new $133,500,000 Academy was being
constructed, the first class of 306 cadets began their
studies in temporary quarters at Lowry Air Force
Base, Denver.

There were, of course, no upperclassmen to "guide"
these freshmen, so the Air Force selected seventy
young officers to act as cadet officers for the first two
years.

The course of study had already been worked out by the late Lieutenant General Hubert Harmon, who became the Academy's first Superintendent. The concept from the beginning was to train leaders who can be as effective at a conference table as in a cockpit. And in early 1958 the Academy established a Department of Astronautics, the first in America.

The curriculum will never remain fixed because man's future in the air is ever changing, but in any event the Air Force is determined that the Academy shall graduate leaders with a broad mental horizon. An Air Force officer is part of a large military organization, but more than in any other branch of our armed services he must also be an individual.

The airman often has to fight alone or in small groups. He must be able to rely on his own resources. What he is taught about himself, his machine, and his world may mean the difference between victory and defeat.

The four-year academic course is divided almost equally between liberal arts and science. The young airman will undoubtedly be part of a highly complex "weapons system" someday and he must know as much as possible about physics, engineering, thermodynamics and scores of other scientific subjects. But to balance these necessary technical studies the cadet will be given a thorough background in the humanities and social sciences such as English, history, psychology, law and philosophy.

In addition to all this, the cadet must also prepare himself for his military profession. The airmanship program at the Academy includes military studies, physical education, and some flying training. During his military training the cadet will visit our bases all over the world. He will also learn aerial navigation in Convair T-29 "flying classrooms" as well as receive preliminary pilot training. (He will have to wait until later to learn to fly.) Upon graduation each cadet is given a bachelor of science degree, a commission as a second lieutenant.

In 1959 the first class of cadets was graduated from the new Academy at Colorado Springs, where Major General Robert H. Warren is now Superintendent. By 1962 the Cadet Wing should reach its total authorized strength of approximately 2,500.

Entrance requirements for the Air Force Academy

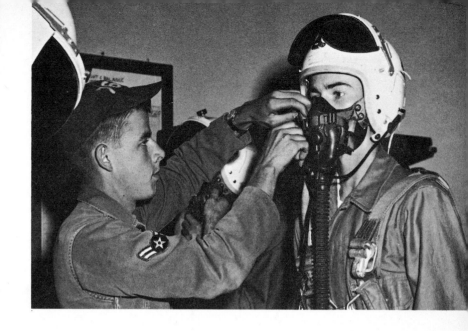

A technician outfits an Air Force Academy cadet for flight in a T-33 jet trainer. (*Below*) The traditional cap tossing takes place following the graduates' last order from the Academy's Commandant of Cadets: "Gentlemen, you are dismissed."

are somewhat similar to those for our two other military academies. Candidates must be between 17 and 22 years of age; they must be citizens of the United States; they must never have been married. The physical standards are high, of course, but they are not as strict as those required for flight training.

In order to compete for admission to the Academy, the would-be cadet must first be nominated by one (or more) of the following nominating authorities:

Congressional. Every United States Senator and Representative is authorized to nominate four candidates. Most of the cadets at the Academy are chosen from this group.

Presidential. The President can nominate eighty-nine sons of members of our armed forces (Air Force, Army, Navy, Marines or Coast Guard).

Regular and Reserve Components. Twelve nominations exist for members of the Regular Components of the Air Force or the Army; and thirteen nominations for members of the Reserve Components of the Air Force, Army, Air National Guard, or National Guard. All of these nominations are filled on a competitive basis.

Sons of Medal of Honor Winners. There is no limit on the number of nominations here. All that is required of the candidate is that he pass the Academy's entrance examinations.

After nomination, the would-be cadet must pass the demanding Air Force Academy Qualifying Medical Examination, the Physical Aptitude Examination, as well as the standard College Entrance Examination Board Tests. The applicant is also judged for character and leadership potential.

The Air Force wants and needs only the best.

The Air Force Academy is new. The Air Force itself is young—in relationship to our other services.

It's young in spirit too. The Air Force is proud of its traditions, but it is not bound by them. Many of its greatest heroes and leaders, even from the earliest days, are still alive. They are men who knew that what they were going to do was more important than what they had already done.

Many Air Force cadets will have the good fortune

to be taught by these men. Others will come under their command after they graduate. These pioneer leaders, these makers of history, have not yet become just a picture on a wall or a chapter of a book. Their lives are still a living inspiration for the "Air Force spirit."

The heritage, then, of the young airman as he enters the Academy is a great one. His own country-men, the Wright brothers, made the first airplane. From then on there is an almost endless list of men of vision and courage, hundreds more than have been mentioned in this book.

In the freshman class now entering the Academy will there be another Rickenbacker, Mitchell, Doo-little, Arnold, Spaatz or LeMay? Will there be any more men like Ben Foulois, Frank Luke, Colin Kelly, Dave Schilling, Don Blakeslee, Dick Bong or Jim Jabara?

There is no doubt about the answer.

Already some of the younger fliers like "Chuck" Yeager, Ivan Kincheloe, and Frank Everest are taking their place in history. The story of the Air Force is just beginning.

Index